Helene Robinson

Basic Piano for Adults

for class and individual instruction

Wadsworth Publishing Company
Belmont, California

THE WADSWORTH MUSIC SERIES

MUSIC LITERATURE

English Folk Song, Fourth Edition by Cecil J. Sharp
The Musical Experience, Second Edition by John Gillespie
The Musical Experience Record Album by John Gillespie
Scored for the Understanding of Music—Supplemented Edition by Charles R. Hoffer and Marjorie Latham Hoffer
Scored for the Understanding of Music Record Album by Charles R. Hoffer
Talking about Symphonies by Antony Hopkins
The Search for Musical Understanding by Robert W. Buggert and Charles B. Fowler
The Understanding of Music, Second Edition by Charles R. Hoffer
The Understanding of Music Record Album by Charles R. Hoffer
The Understanding of Music Enrichment Record Album by Charles R. Hoffer

MUSIC FOUNDATIONS

Basic Concepts in Music by Gary M. Martin
Basic Resources for Learning Music, Second Edition by Alice Snyder Knuth and William E. Knuth
Foundations in Music Theory, Second Edition with Programed Exercises by Leon Dallin
Introduction to Musical Understanding and Musicianship by Ethel G. Adams
Music Essentials by Robert Pace

MUSIC SKILLS

Advanced Music Reading by William Thomson
Basic Piano for Adults by Helene Robinson
Intermediate Piano for Adults, Volume I by Helene Robinson
Intermediate Piano for Adults, Volume II by Helene Robinson
Introduction to Ear Training by William Thomson and Richard P. DeLone
Introduction to Music Reading by William Thomson
Keyboard Harmony: A Comprehensive Approach to Musicianship by Isabel Lehmer
Keyboard Skills: Sight Reading, Transposition, Harmonization, Improvisation by Winifred K. Chastek
Master Themes for Sight Singing and Dictation by Winifred K. Chastek
Music Dictation: A Stereo-Taped Series by Robert G. Olson
Music Literature for Analysis and Study by Charles W. Walton
Steps to Singing for Voice Classes by Royal Stanton

MUSIC THEORY

Harmony and Melody, Volume I: The Diatonic Style by Elie Siegmeister
Harmony and Melody, Volume II: Modulation; Chromatic and Modern Styles by Elie Siegmeister
A Workbook for Harmony and Melody, Volume I by Elie Siegmeister
A Workbook for Harmony and Melody, Volume II by Elie Siegmeister

MUSIC EDUCATION

A Concise Introduction to Teaching Elementary School Music by William O. Hughes
Exploring Music with Children by Robert E. Nye and Vernice T. Nye
Music in the Education of Children, Third Edition by Bessie R. Swanson
Singing with Children, Second Edition by Robert E. Nye, Vernice T. Nye, Neva Aubin, and George Kyme
Teaching Music in the Secondary Schools, Second Edition by Charles R. Hoffer

28 — 97 96

L.C. Cat. Card No.: 64-15485

Printed in the United States of America

ISBN 0-534-00065-7

PREFACE

This book is the outcome of the author's years of experience in teaching and testing materials and methods with individual students and classes of beginners.

The book is designed for students majoring in elementary education or in music, and for any adult or teen-age beginner on the piano. A complete course for early piano study, the book provides for the acquisition of basic skills in playing and reading music, and presents the fundamentals of musical theory and structure. Included are pieces or studies employing all phases of technique needed to play piano literature of easy to intermediate level.

The music has been selected to appeal to adult interest, and is carefully arranged in progressive order of technical difficulty. In this one volume there is a varied repertoire of folk songs and short classical, romantic, and contemporary compositions, suitable for use in the classroom and in the home.

Simple familiar songs in five-finger position are presented first by rote, to enable the student to acquire familiarity with the keyboard, associate pitch with keys and fingers, and gain some finger facility. New topics and techniques are introduced one at a time to simplify the learning. Theory is presented functionally, each aspect being applied immediately in music that is played. Follow-up pieces reinforce the learning.

Other features include analysis of musical structure as an aid to playing, reading, and understanding music; suggestions to guide student practice; written assignments for independent student work; transposition; creative activities, including harmonization; an abundance of material to permit selection for individual needs; a glossary of musical terms; and a classified index.

ACKNOWLEDGMENTS

The author wishes to thank the piano classes that have tested the materials of this book and the many persons, too numerous to mention, who have read the manuscript and contributed ideas and encouragement. Special thanks go to Mrs. Aurora Underwood of Portland State College in Oregon, Dr. William Richards of San Fernando State College in California, Dr. Leslie Clausen of Los Angeles City College, Dr. Robert Nye of the University of Oregon, Dr. Frederick Owens of Chico State College in California, Miss Jessie Lee Thompson, editor at Wadsworth Publishing Company, and to my parents, Dr. and Mrs. K. K. Robinson.

Gratitude is expressed to the publishers and authors for permission to use the following materials in this book:

American Book Company, for "Pat Works on the Railway," and for "Hawaiian Night," both from The American Singer, Book 5, revised edition by Beattie, Wolverton, Wilson, and Hinga, copyright 1955.

Boosey and Hawkes, Inc., for "Evening in the Country," by Béla Bartók, from "Ten Easy Pieces for Piano."

Leeds Music Corporation, for "The Clown" (Op. 39), by Dmitri Kabalevsky, edited and annotated by Alfred Mirovitch, © copyright MCMXLVIII by Leeds Music Corporation, New York, N. Y., used by permission, all rights reserved.

Planetary Music Publishing Corporation, for the melody of "The Yellow Rose of Texas," by Don George, copyright 1955.

PRELIMINARY CONSIDERATIONS FOR THE STUDENT

1. Regular daily practice is essential for the development of muscular skill. For most beginners, two periods of twenty-five to thirty minutes each are more effective than a one-hour practice period. Each day, review a few pieces that you have already learned.

2. Two lessons a week are recommended for the first two weeks of study, if possible, to prevent the formation of incorrect habits.

3. At the piano, sit directly in front of the center of the keyboard, on a bench of proper height to bring elbows at key level, and at a distance that permits freedom of arm movement. Maintain good posture; keep feet flat on the floor. Avoid tension in the shoulders and wrists.

4. Use favorable hand position, which your teacher will demonstrate (arched hands, curved fingers, short nails so fingers can play on the tips). One way to attain correct position is to drop the relaxed hands, palms up, onto the lap, where the fingers naturally curl. Then, lift one hand at a time, gently turn it over without altering its shape, and place it on the keyboard, with each finger resting on an adjacent white key. Do this several times a day to acquire a good habit.

THE PIANO KEYBOARD

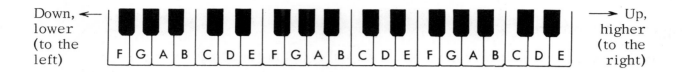

Down, ← lower (to the left)

→ Up, higher (to the right)

The first seven letters of the alphabet—A B C D E F G—are used over and over to name the keys of the piano.

The black keys serve as signposts. Observe the alternating groups of two and three black keys. The white key between two black keys is D. Find all the D's on your piano. How can you distinguish between F and C? Find several F's, several C's. Find other keys dictated by your teacher.

Middle C is the C nearest the center of the piano keyboard. Find it. From one C to the next C above or below is an octave (meaning "eight")—the distance from one key to the next key with the same name. Play several octaves.

Learn the names of all the white keys within an octave, and you will know all the keys on the piano. Practice one minute twice daily, until you can instantly identify any key. How fast can you say the musical alphabet backward?

PITCH AND MELODY

Pitch refers to how high or how low a musical tone is. Play a high tone and a low tone on your piano.

A melody is a tune made of varying pitches (tones that move up, down, or repeat). Sing "Merrily We Roll Along" and show with your hand how the tune moves to different pitch levels, as illustrated:

                                                          a-long;
    Mer-   roll a-long,   roll
        ri- we   roll a-long,
            ly

    Mer-   roll a-long,   deep
        ri- we   o'er the   blue
            ly   sea.

FINGER NUMBERS

Learn the finger numbers pictured here. As the teacher calls each number, play the correct finger number in the air. Practice this with each hand, then with both together.

LEFT   RIGHT

1

THREE ROTE SONGS

Play these familiar songs by finger number and position on the keys, to develop some finger control and familiarity with the keyboard.

Suggested Procedure:

1. Sing the song to refresh your memory of it, and clap the rhythm.

2. Sing the right-hand finger numbers (printed above the music), and play the right-hand fingers in the air.

3. Place the right-hand fingers on the keys in the FINGER POSITION illustrated for the song. Keep each finger over its own key. Sing and play by finger number only, disregarding the names of keys and notes while you are playing.

4. Sing the left-hand finger numbers (printed below the music). Sing and play left-hand fingers first in the air, then on the keys in the position illustrated.

5. Observe that the notes in the music show how the tune moves—down, up, or on the same pitch level.

6. On the finger-position charts, name the keys played. Play these keys rapidly, ascending and descending, to develop dexterity and a "feel" for the position.

FINGER POSITION for "Merrily We Roll Along"

1. MERRILY WE ROLL ALONG

Play Song 1 in this FINGER POSITION using finger 3 on the black key to the right of F.

Finger numbers for the black keys are printed above the black keys on the keyboards.

2

TRANSPOSITION

To play a song in a different key (position) is called transposing. You have transposed Song 1 into the key of D major. Now transpose it by starting it on B (key of G major), then on A (key of F major); both positions are illustrated on this page.

FINGER POSITION
for
Song 2.

2. JINGLE BELLS

J. S. Pierpont (1785-1866)

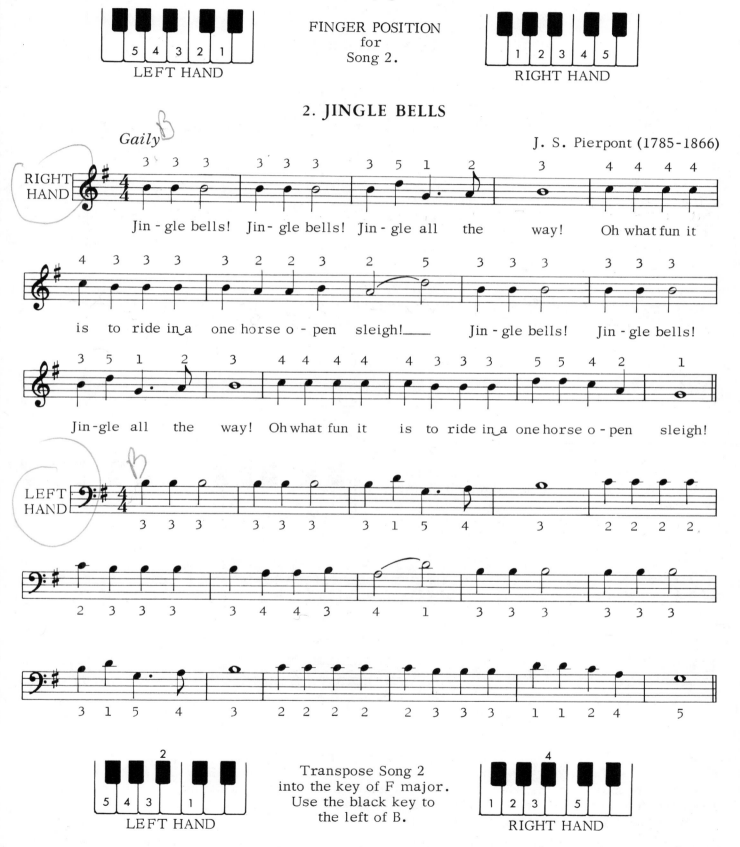

Transpose Song 2 into the key of F major. Use the black key to the left of B.

Transpose Song 2 into the key of A major; 3rd fingers play the black key to the right of C.

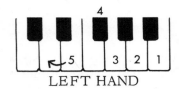

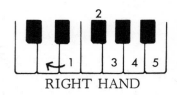

FINGER POSITION
for Song 3.
The right-hand thumb and
left-hand 5th finger do
double duty; for the final
tone they move down
from E to D.

3. LONDON BRIDGE

Lively

English

Lon - don Bridge is fall - ing down, fall - ing down, fall - ing down,

Lon - don Bridge is fall - ing down, My fair la - dy.

Song 3 transposed. Study the new finger position. Remember to reach down to C for the final tone.

R. H. = right hand; L. H. = left hand.

FROM ROTE TO NOTE

Each note of music on the page represents a tone or key to play on the piano. The note and the key have the same letter name. If you sing the key names as you play, you will also be singing the letter names of the notes. You might try this.

Hereafter, finger numbers will not be given for every note of a song. Songs will be learned by reading the notes.

4

NOTATION OF PITCH

Notes are written on the lines and in the spaces of the STAFF. Count the 5 lines and 4 spaces from the lowest up to the highest. The line-space-line-space arrangement makes the nine STAFF DEGREES.

The TREBLE STAFF is indicated by the TREBLE or G CLEF sign, which encircles the second staff line and locates on it the first G above Middle C. In general, the treble staff is for right-hand notes from Middle C upward. Find the illustrated note on your piano.

The BASS STAFF is indicated by the BASS or F CLEF 𝄢 sign, which designates the fourth staff line as the first F below Middle C (see dots). In general, the bass staff is for left-hand notes from Middle C downward. Find the illustrated note on your piano.

The GRAND or GREAT STAFF combines treble and bass staffs (staves), making, in effect, an eleven-line staff, with the middle line used only as a LEGER LINE.* Observe that Middle C, between the staffs, may be used either as a treble note or as a bass note. Why do the corresponding lines and spaces of the two staffs have different letter names?

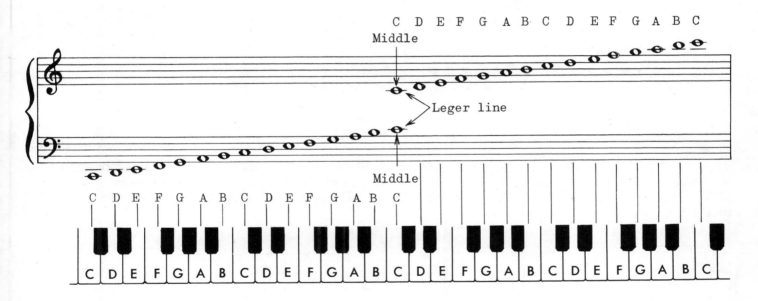

Observe that every STAFF DEGREE (every line and space) has a letter name, and that the name corresponds to the name of a white key on the piano.

Beginning on Middle C with the right hand, play and name all the treble notes on the grand staff, ascending, then descending. Begin on Middle C with the left hand, and name and play all the bass notes, descending and then ascending.

Memorize the note names immediately. Avoid "crutches" that impose an additional mental process. Until you are able to identify notes instantly, say the letter name of each treble and bass note before and after you play a song. Do not always name notes while playing because the process retards the playing and hinders reading by intervals; but name the notes sometimes, to develop association of note and key names.

What are the names of the treble and bass notes of Songs 1 and 2?

WRITING PRACTICE: Written Assignment One, page 9. Fill in II and III.

---

*Leger lines (also spelled ledger) are short lines added for notes above or below the treble or bass staff. Find leger lines in the diagram of the grand staff.

LEGATO TOUCH. Connect the tones smoothly, but avoid blurring two tones together (compare the process with walking). Always listen to the effect while you play; make legato tones "sing."

4. EXERCISES in FIVE-FINGER POSITION (Key of C Major)

Practice each hand alone for speed and evenness of tones; then try both hands together. Use the favorable hand position (see "Preliminary Considerations," p. iv). Transpose into other keys.

(i) FIVE-FINGER PATTERN

(ii) TWO FINGERS WALKING

(iii) ARPEGGIO

Arpa is Italian for harp. Play the 1st, 3rd, and 5th notes (C-E-G) of the five-finger pattern on four successive octave ranges, alternating hands. These three notes are skips—every other key played by every other finger. Move your hands in the air to feel the movement; say "left-right," then finger numbers, then key names.

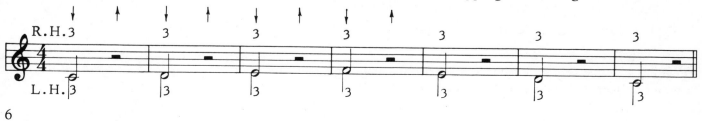

(iv) EXERCISE for ARM FREEDOM (Optional)

Lift the arm, leading with the wrist, dangling the finger tips three inches above key level. Drop the arm weight onto the 3rd finger, making the first (nail) joint firm and curving the finger and hand into correct position as the finger depresses the key. Lift the hand and arm, leading with the wrist. Repeat on the next note. The arrows indicate the dropping and lifting action.

AIDS TO NOTE READING

1. Watch the music and not your hands or the keys as you play.

2. Try to see at a glance a group of notes, not just one note at a time.

3. Within this group, perceive the <u>direction</u> (up, down, same) and the <u>distance</u> (number of staff degrees) between notes.

   If the next note is one staff degree higher or lower (on the next letter of the alphabet), use the adjacent finger to play the adjacent key above or below.

   If the next note skips a staff degree (skips a letter of the alphabet), skip a finger and a key. Motto: "Skip a letter, skip a finger."

Study and play the following examples, first with the right hand, then with the left.

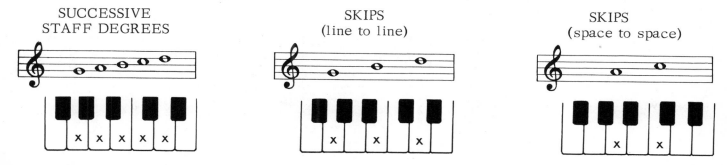

Write the finger number for the second note of each example below. Play the examples.

Procedure for Song 5:

1. Hear the song (sung and played by the teacher).
2. Sing the song and clap the rhythm as you listen again.
3. Find how many notes move in the same direction on successive staff degrees, and the number and distance of skips. Find any repetition in the music.
4. Use the five-finger pattern for position, right thumb on C, left 5th finger on C. Plan the fingering for the successive notes and for the skipping notes. Observe the clef signs.
5. Play the song rhythmically with the right hand, then with the left, reading the notes by staff degrees up or down.
6. After you play the song well several times, sing the names of the notes as you play.

5. WE CAN PLAY THE MUSIC

Lively   German (arr. H. R.)

We can play the mu-sic, mu-sic, mu-sic; We can play the mu-sic, Hear us as we play.

Transpose into the key of G major. Start on G; read up and down by staff degrees. Transpose into the key of A major, using 3rd fingers on the black key to the right of C.

Songs 6, 7, and 8: Sing the song and clap the rhythm. Learn the rhythm by ear; do not count the time now. Find your finger position, observing the highest and lowest notes to be played. Plan your fingering.

Be sure to watch the music and not your hands as you play.

Song 6. Learn each hand separately; later, play both hands in unison. When you can play Song 6 with ease, transpose it into other keys. Start on the third finger.

6. GO TELL AUNT RHODIE

American

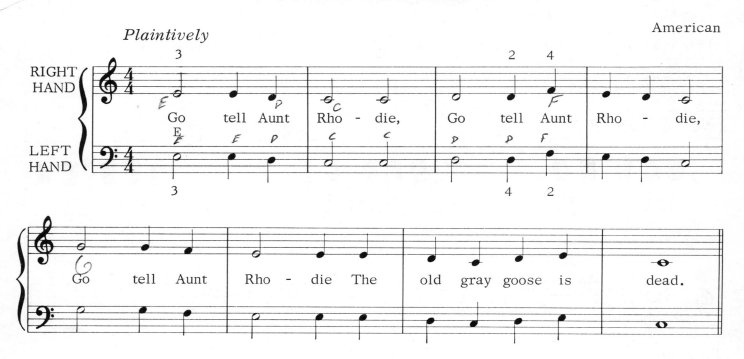

Song 7. Position as for the key of C major. Key signatures will be explained later. Sing the song and clap the rhythm. Play the rhythm by ear.

7. ALL THROUGH THE NIGHT (Excerpt)

Welsh

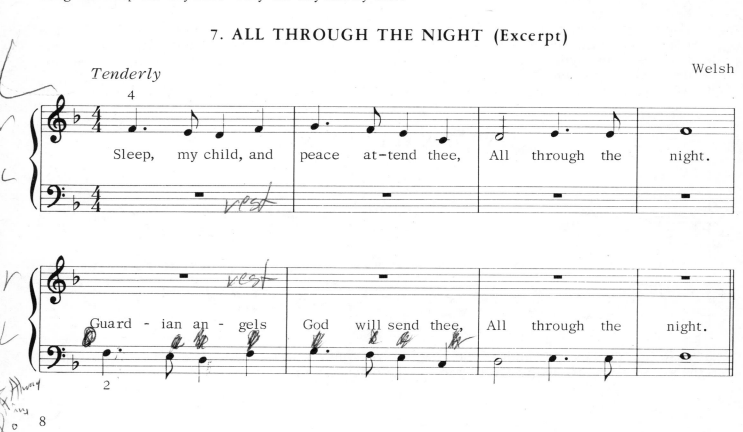

8

Song 8. Position as for the key of C major.

8. AURA LEE

George Poulton

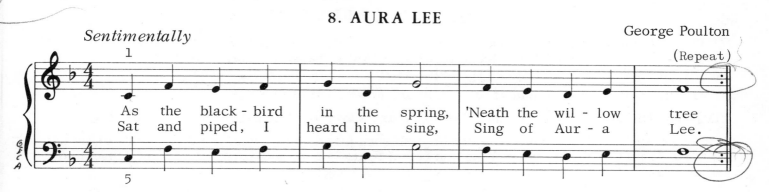

Sentimentally

As   the   black - bird   in   the   spring,   'Neath the   wil - low   tree
Sat   and   piped,   I   heard him   sing,   Sing   of   Aur - a   Lee.

WRITTEN ASSIGNMENT ONE

I.   1. The treble clef locates the pitch____ on the ____ line of the staff.
     2. The bass clef locates the pitch ____ on the ____ line of the staff.
     3. Trace the process of making a treble clef. Observe distances and exact crossing of
        lines. Make three complete treble clefs, then two bass clefs.

II. 1. On the blanks beneath each note, write the letter name (pitch) of the note.

     2. Draw the indicated note above each letter.

        C   G   D   A   F   B   E   C   G   D   A   F   B   E

III. On the treble staff below, write these notes and fill in their letter names. Count each new
     note from the preceding note:

        A note on the G line.
        A note one staff degree higher.
        A higher note that skips one staff degree.
        A note one staff degree lower.
        A lower note that skips two staff degrees.

        G   ___   ___   ___   ___   D   ___   ___   ___   ___

IV. On the bass staff above, write the following notes and fill in their letter names:

        A note on the D line.
        A note one staff degree lower.
        A higher note that skips one staff degree.
        A higher note that skips two staff degrees.
        A lower note that skips one staff degree.

KEYBOARD DRILL: How fast can you locate keys dictated by another person?

9

NOTATION OF RHYTHM

METER. Music, like poetry, has meter—a regular recurring pattern of strong and weak beats (pulsations). Vertical BAR LINES (MEASURE BARS) mark the staff into MEASURES, which usually start on a strong beat and usually have the same number of beats.

A DOUBLE BAR marks the end of the music or of a section of music.

TIME VALUES. The relative lengths of tones are shown by the kinds of notes and rests.

Sing and clap "Hot Cross Buns," the old English song given below, and find three kinds of rhythm: (1) the accents (strong beats); (2) the number of beats in each measure; and (3) the longest notes and shortest notes. How many measures are in the song?

Hot cross buns!   Hot cross buns!   One a pen-ny, two a pen-ny, Hot cross buns!

COUNT: 1   2   3   4   1   2   3   4   1 & 2 & 3 & 4 &   1   2   3   4

TIME (METER) SIGNATURE—the two numbers (not fractions) at the beginning of the music.

Upper number is the number of beats in a measure.
$\frac{}{4}$ indicates four beats in a measure.

Lower number tells what kind of note receives one beat.
$\overline{4}$ stands for a quarter note (or its equivalent).

$\mathbf{C} = \frac{4}{4}$ (Common Time)   ¢ $= \frac{2}{2}$ *Alla Breve* (Cut Time)

PARTS OF NOTES: Head ο ; with Stem ♩ ; with Flag ♪ ; with Beam ♫

TIME VALUES OF NOTES AND RESTS

Kind of Note	Corresponding Rest	Number of Beats in $\frac{4}{4}$ Meter	Portion of the Measure	Sample Measure 1	2	3	4
whole	▬	4 beats	whole measure	ο			
half	▬	2 beats	one-half	♩		♩	
quarter	ξ ʑ	1 beat	one-fourth	♩	♩	♩	♩
eighth	٧	½ beat	one-eighth				
2 eighths		total one beat		♫	♫	♫	♫
sixteenth	٧	¼ beat	one-sixteenth				
4 sixteenths		total one beat					

A DOT lengthens the preceding note by half the value of the note (the dot receives half as much time as the note). In $\frac{4}{4}$ time ♩. $= 1\frac{1}{2}$ beats, ♩. $= 3$ beats.

WAYS OF "KEEPING TIME":
Clapping before playing. Clap each note; shake the clasped hands once for each extra beat (e.g., ♩ =clap, shake; ο =clap, shake, shake, shake).
Tapping the beat with the left heel while playing.
It is traditional to count the beats in each measure while playing.
    Count the beats aloud and play the notes of "Hot Cross Buns," above.
Beginners find it helpful to chant (rhythmically) the time values of the notes, as follows:

quar-ter   quar-ter   half note   quar-ter   two eighths   quar-ter   dot   eighth

Clap the notes of Song 6, page 8. Then play and count the beats in each measure.

PATTERNS

A musical pattern (or motive) is a recognizable figure or design formed by a group of notes. The pattern may be melodic or rhythmic or both. A pattern usually occurs more than once and helps give the music its particular character and individuality. The recognition of patterns is an aid to reading, playing, interpreting, and memorizing music. Try to read an entire pattern as one unit, not separate notes. In Song 9, find a pattern that occurs twice.

Song 9. Position: key of G major; G A B C D for each hand. Play the five-finger pattern. Plan the fingering for each hand, observing the skips. Clap the notes and chant the time values. Play each hand alone, counting the beats in each measure. After each hand plays well, try both hands in unison. How many measures are in Song 9?

Transpose this song into the key of F major, playing the black key to the left of B.

9. J'AI DU BON TABAC

French

SLUR:

A SLUR (curved line above or below a group of two or more notes) indicates that these notes are to be played legato. Read the slurred notes as a unit; slightly shorten and soften the last note of the unit.

The exercise below is especially helpful in learning how to play slurs.

10. EXERCISE for WRIST FLEXIBILITY, ARM FREEDOM, and FIRM FINGER JOINTS

↓ = Drop,
↑ = Lift,
the wrist.

Songs 11 and 12. Find the repeated tonal-rhythmic patterns; chant the time values of notes in these groups and also in unlike measures. Before playing, count one measure. Continue to count while you play.

<u>Keep each finger over its own key.</u>

Song 11. Finger position: both thumbs on Middle C.

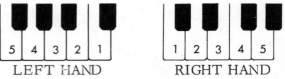

11. LET US BE MERRY

Czech and Polish

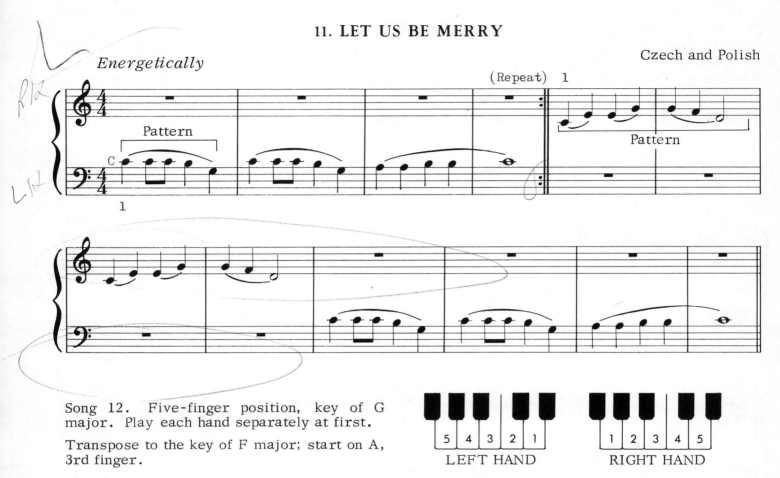

Song 12. Five-finger position, key of G major. Play each hand separately at first.

Transpose to the key of F major; start on A, 3rd finger.

12. SCHLAF, KINDLEIN, SCHLAF

German Lullaby

12

PIECES FOR SIGHT READING

Clap and chant the note values. Find your position on the keys. Play and count the time.

(1) THE COBBLER, Bavarian

Vigorously

(2) SUNNY SKIES (H. R.)

With a swing

(3) GAME SONG, Chilean

Quickly

(4) AUTUMN SHOWERS, German

Moderately fast

*Repeat the first four measures of this song.

WRITTEN ASSIGNMENT TWO

I. Time (Meter) Signature, and Note Values

1. In the meter or time signature, the upper number indicates _____
_____ ; the lower number indicates _____
_____ .

2. Identify the kind of note and indicate the number of beats it receives.

Kind : _____ _____ _____ _____ _____ _____ _____

Beats: _____ _____ _____ _____ _____ _____ _____

II. Equivalents

Each blank line below indicates the length of one note. Fill in the missing notes.

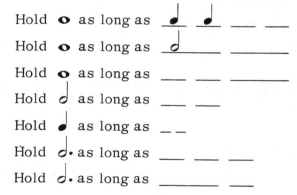

III. Stem Placement on Notes

Stems usually point up (on the right) on notes below the middle line of the staff, and down (on the left) on notes on or above the middle line. Flags are always on the right of the stem.

On this staff, draw stems on all the notes. Add flags to the last two notes.

RHYTHM ACTIVITY

COUNT the beats of each measure and CLAP the notes (see "Ways of Keeping Time," p. 10).

C MAJOR CHORD ACCOMPANIMENT

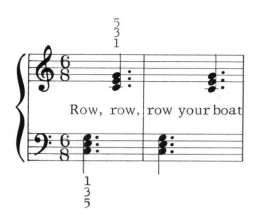

The three notes of the arpeggio (C-E-G), played simultaneously, make the C major chord. Play the chords, crossing hands as for the arpeggio.

Sing "Row, Row, Row Your Boat," starting on C, and clap two beats per measure. Sing again, and play the chord accompaniment, alternating hands as shown on this staff. ("Row, row, row your boat, gently down the stream; Merrily, merrily, merrily, merrily, life is but a dream.")

As an accompaniment for "We Can Play the Music" (Song 5, page 7), play a C major chord at the beginning of each measure, playing left-hand chords for the right-hand melody, right-hand chords for the left-hand melody, as illustrated.

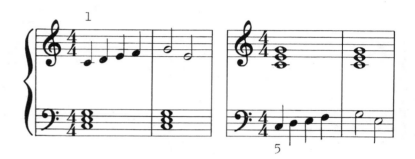

TONIC(I) AND DOMINANT SEVENTH(V₇) CHORDS
(Key of C Major)

Many songs can be harmonized with only two chords—the TONIC CHORD (Chord I), and the DOMINANT SEVENTH CHORD (Chord V₇). The C major chord, which you made from the arpeggio and played with the song above, is the tonic chord in the key of C major.

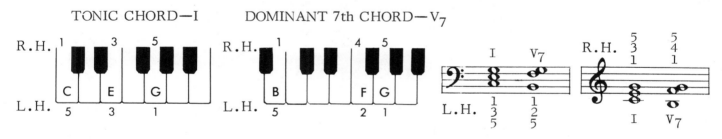

Play the V₇ chord several times to get the "feel" of it.

FORMULA for moving from Chord I to Chord V₇:

This same formula can be used when playing in any key.

Practice these chords with each hand until you can shift quickly from one chord to the other.

Play chords dictated by the teacher.

The structure of chords will be explained on page 33.

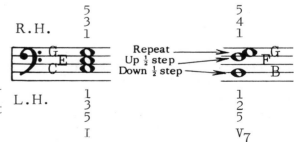

HALF STEP

A HALF STEP is the closest distance on the piano. From any key to the next one (black or white) is a half step. (Play several half-steps.)

15

Song 13. Play the chords while another person plays the melody in DUET. Then play the melody and chords simultaneously, yourself.

13. MERRILY WE ROLL ALONG

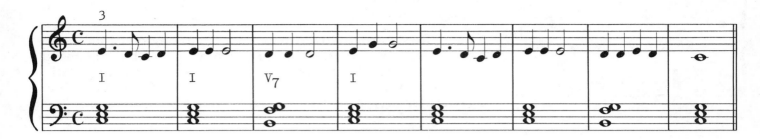

Play "Go Tell Aunt Rhodie" (page 8) with chords. Play and write one chord per measure on beat "1" in this order: I I V$_7$ I, I I V$_7$ I.

SCALE AND KEY

Play the C major scale—the eight white keys in succession from one C to the next. Since the "home tone" (name note) is C, this scale is called the C scale. A song that uses the tones of this scale and comes to repose (concludes) on C is in the key of C major. Other scales require sharps or flats. You have already transposed some songs from one key to another, using one or more sharps or flats. The structure of scales is explained on page 30.

SHARPS AND FLATS

A SHARP (♯) raises the pitch of a note a half step to the closest key above.
A FLAT (♭) lowers the pitch of a note a half step to the closest key below.

    Find on the piano: F♯, G♭, C♯, D♭, B♭, G♯.

    Find and name the key: one half step above B, E, A, D;
                           one half step below F, C, B, E.

KEY SIGNATURES OF MAJOR KEYS

The KEY SIGNATURE at the beginning of each staff lists the sharps and flats we must remember to play. It also enables us to find the KEYNOTE (home tone) of the key in which the music is written; this helps us find our playing position.

How to find the keynote, using the key signature:

In sharps, the keynote is one note above the last sharp.
In flats, the keynote has the same name as the next-to-the-last flat.

Key of G

Key of E♭

Remember: the key of C major has no sharps or flats; the key of F major has one flat.

16

14. EXERCISES and CHORDS (Key of G Major)

FIVE-FINGER PATTERN   CHORDS   ARPEGGIO

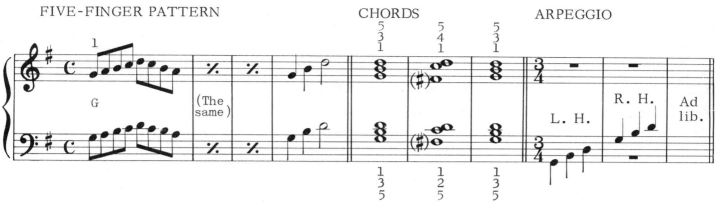

F sharp occurs in the V_7 chord, but is not within the range of the five-finger pattern.
The formula for moving from Chord I to Chord V_7 (p. 15) applies in all keys.

REST — silence for the duration of the equivalent note value. Learn these rests:

▬ whole   ▬ half   𝄽 quarter   𝄾 eighth

D.C. AL FINE — go back to the beginning (Da Capo — the "head"), and repeat the music to Fine (Fee-nay), the end or finish.

Song 15. Observe the key and time signature (cut time). Sing and clap two beats per measure. Play the dotted rhythm by ear in measures 3 and 7. Practice the Preparatory Exercise. How far below its original position does the right-hand thumb move? Prepare the right thumb over E before the left hand begins to play its melody.

15. ALOUETTE

Gaily   French-Canadian

17

$\frac{2}{4}$ METER—two beats in a measure; a quarter note receives one beat.

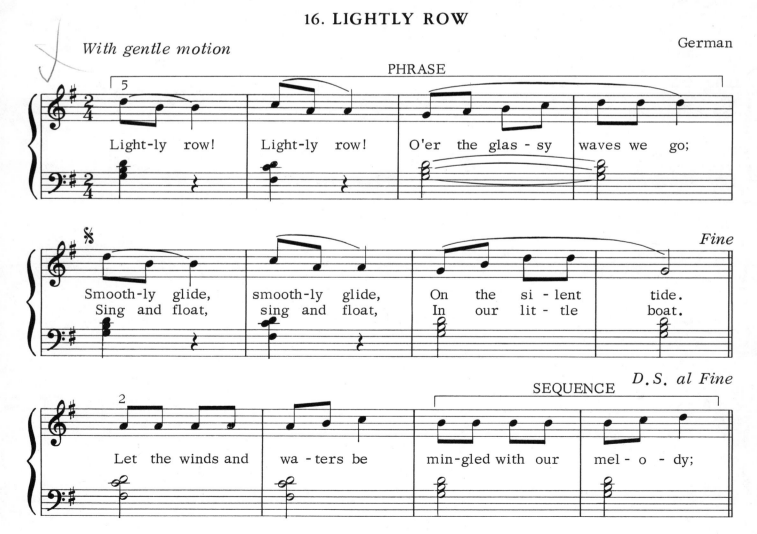

TIE—a curved line connects two notes of the same pitch, making a single continuous sound for the duration of both notes.

D.S. (DAL SEGNO)—repeat from the sign 𝄋 ; stop at Fine.

SEQUENCE—a tonal pattern that is repeated at a higher or lower pitch (e.g. the first two measures of "Lightly Row").

THE PHRASE

A phrase is a unit of structure in music comparable to a line of poetry or to a sentence. A phrase ends on a cadence or point of repose that provides a breathing place in the music. The pianist, like the singer, should "breathe" (with his fingers) at the end of a phrase. This act of PHRASING in music, like punctuation in language, is important in conveying meaning. In simple music, phrases are usually four measures long, but may vary. A phrase may contain several PHRASE MEMBERS (patterns or slurred groups). Often these units of design are important enough to be "phrased" or separated, also. Phrasing should not interrupt the rhythmic flow.

In Song 16 distinguish between phrases and phrase members. Find the number of phrases; compare them in length, melody, and rhythm. Find three sequences, a five-finger pattern, and a tonic chord pattern in the melody. How many different one-measure rhythm patterns do you find? During the "rests," prepare the fingers for the next chord.

16. LIGHTLY ROW

German

With gentle motion

Light-ly row! Light-ly row! O'er the glas - sy waves we go;

Smooth-ly glide, smooth-ly glide, On the si - lent tide.
Sing and float, sing and float, In our lit - tle boat.

Let the winds and wa - ters be min-gled with our mel - o - dy;

16a.

17. EXERCISES, CHORDS, and ARPEGGIOS (Key of F Major)

DYNAMICS

The term dynamics refers to the degrees of intensity or volume of tones, which are varied to make the music more expressive.

Analyze the use of dynamics to achieve drama in Song 18.

Here are some common dynamic marks:

p = piano (soft) mf = mezzo forte (moderately loud)

mp = mezzo piano (moderately soft) f = forte (loud)

crescendo (cresc.) or ⟨———— = gradual increase in volume

diminuendo (dim.) or ————⟩ = gradual decrease in volume

Song 18. Observe the time signature. Clap the rhythm of the first two measures. How many times is this rhythm pattern repeated? Observe the key signature; play the keynote and the flat. In the melody, find the tonic-chord pattern; a three-note pattern on adjacent staff degrees; and repeated patterns. In what order do the chords progress?

18. LOVE SOMEBODY

American (arr. H. R.)

20

$\frac{3}{4}$ METER—3 beats in a measure.

Song 19 is easy to read. Find the number of phrases, ties, and melody notes on the bass staff; find a treble note that extends one note below the five-finger position. Transpose the song.

19. DOWN IN THE VALLEY

American

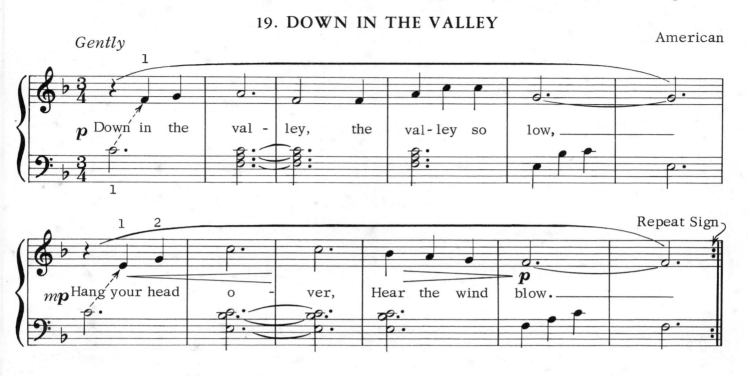

INTERVALS

An interval is the distance on the staff covered by two notes in a melody or in a chord. To measure an interval, count the number of staff degrees (lines and spaces) involved, including the staff degrees on which both notes are written. Remember to call the starting note number "1," not zero. Examples:

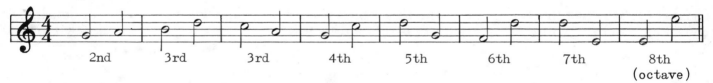

2nd   3rd   3rd   4th   5th   6th   7th   8th
                                                              (octave)

Learn to recognize intervals quickly on the staff and on the keyboard.

Identify intervals in the melody of Songs 19, 21, and 22. Say "up a 3rd, down a 4th," etc.

Play intervals from a given note dictated by your teacher.

Complete section V of Written Assignment Three (p. 23).

20. EXERCISES and CHORDS (Key of D Major)

Play the chords
in arpeggio form.

TEMPO means rate of speed. Tempo affects the expressive character of music. Tempo markings (usually in Italian) are given above the first staff on the left. (The Glossary lists common Italian tempo marks in order from the slowest to the fastest.)

Song 21. Find where the melody goes down onto the bass staff and where it extends above the five-finger pattern; <u>shift</u> finger position at the <u>encircled</u> finger number. When bass and treble notes move in the same direction, what color of keys are together?

Play the melody of Song 21 as a ROUND with another person. One person plays an octave higher than the written notes; the other person plays an octave lower and starts two measures after the first player. Count aloud to stay together.

21. ARE YOU SLEEPING?

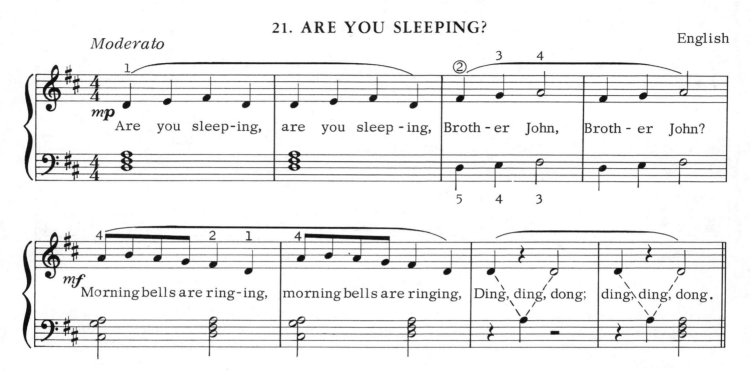

22. THIS OLD MAN

Song 22. Why use the 4th finger on the first note? Find in the melody the tonic-chord notes in the opening pattern, two five-finger patterns from a different note, bass and treble notes that move in the same direction (notice which fingers play the black keys), and sixteenth notes ($\sqcup\!\!\sqcup$ = 1 beat). Check the intervals to plan the fingering.

WRITTEN ASSIGNMENT THREE

I. Below each note on the treble staff, write the name of the note. On the bass staff write notes that are one octave below each note on the treble staff.

II. 1. Add one note to make the correct number of beats in each measure:

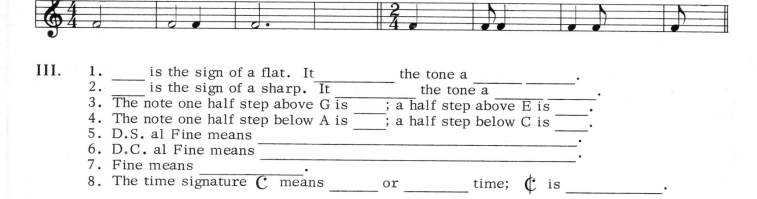

III. 1. ____ is the sign of a flat. It _____ the tone a _____ _____.
    2. ____ is the sign of a sharp. It _____ the tone a _____ _____.
    3. The note one half step above G is ____; a half step above E is ____.
    4. The note one half step below A is ____; a half step below C is ____.
    5. D.S. al Fine means _____.
    6. D.C. al Fine means _____.
    7. Fine means _____.
    8. The time signature C means ____ or _____ time; ₵ is _____.

IV. 1. Write the key indicated by the following key signatures (see rule p. 16):

Key of ____   Key of ____   Key of ____   Key of ____   Chord I   Chord I

    2. On the bass staff above, write the tonic chord in the keys given.

V. 1. Identify these intervals:

    2. On the keyboard below, write the name of each key that is touched by the curving line.

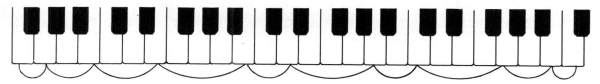

    3. Below each curve, write the kind of interval made between points where the keys are touched.

KEYBOARD REVIEW

Within 10 seconds, locate in a one-octave range on the piano the following keys in the given order and in reverse order: E, C, G, D, B, F, A, F♯, B♭, C♯.

In 15 seconds, with eyes closed, find these dictated keys: F, C, E, A, D, G, B, C♯, F♯, B♭.

PICKUP or UPBEAT: The piece starts with a portion of a measure; each phrase usually begins and ends at a corresponding point in its measure for symmetry of design.

ACCENT > =stress or emphasis on the note marked.

Find repetition of patterns in Song 23. Practice each pattern several times. Slurs in the following song show two notes sung to one syllable of text.

PREPARATORY EXERCISE:
(Extension of Position)

23. I'M TRAMPIN'

Spiritual (arr. H. R.)

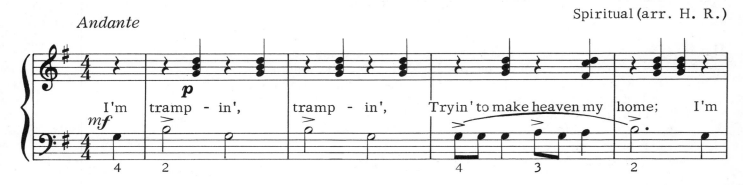

24

REPEAT the music from the beginning.

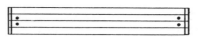 REPEAT the music between the signs.

THE SUBDOMINANT (IV) CHORD

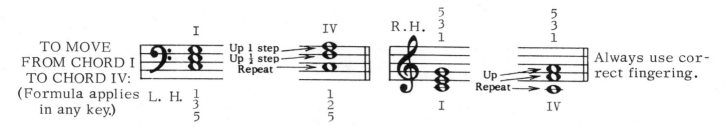

TO MOVE FROM CHORD I TO CHORD IV: (Formula applies in any key.)

Up 1 step
Up ½ step
Repeat

R.H.

Up
Repeat

Always use correct fingering.

Practice Exercise 24 with each hand separately. Memorize it. Transpose it. To ensure precision, anticipate the shape of the chord in the fingers, and touch the keys of each new chord an instant before playing. Learn to shift quickly.

24. EXERCISE: CHORD PROGRESSIONS

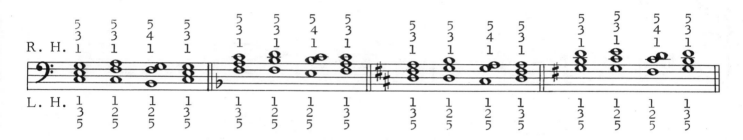

Song 25. Play the chords indicated by Roman numerals below each measure. At the encircled finger numbers in the melody, extend a finger or shift the hand to a new position. Count "1 and 2 and"; begin on the "and" of beat "2." Tap two beats per measure with your left heel as you play. Play the dotted rhythm by ear (𝄾 = ½ beat).

25. OH! SUSANNA

Gaily

Stephen Foster (1826-1864)

I___ came from Al - a - ba - ma With my ban - jo on my knee, I'm ___
It___ rained all night the day I left, The weath-er it was dry, The ___

goin' to Loui - si - an - a, My_____ true love for to see.
sun so hot I froze to death, Su - san - na, don't you cry.
D.S. goin' to Loui - si - an - a With my ban - jo on my knee.

Oh! Su - san - na, oh, don't you cry for me; For I'm

25

$\frac{6}{8}$ METER — 6 beats in a measure, ♪ receives one beat.

Accent the first beat of each half of the measure (beats 1 and 4), conveying a feeling of only two beats per measure in fast $\frac{6}{8}$ meter, or a lilt in slower tempo.

COUNT and CLAP these measures:

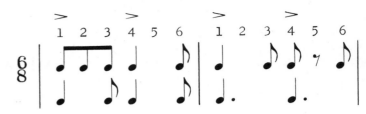

Notice that ♩ ♪♩ ♪ is a "skipping" rhythm (long-short, long-short).

The eighth rest, of course, receives a different time duration in $\frac{6}{8}$ than in $\frac{4}{4}$.

Song 26. Find the keynote; touch the sharp keys. Play the five-finger pattern and chords. Do any repeated patterns form a sequence? Count the time as you play.

26. FOR HE'S A JOLLY GOOD FELLOW

Old French Tune "Marlboro"

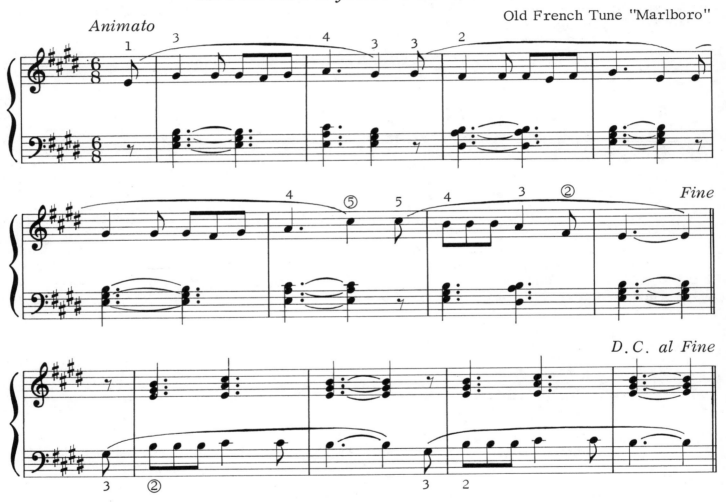

27. EXERCISE for WRIST FLEXIBILITY, ARM FREEDOM, and FIRM FINGERS

↓ = "drop," ↑ = "lift."
Quick tempo, two beats per measure.

Transpose this exercise into the key of E Major.

WAYS OF CHANGING FINGER POSITION SMOOTHLY

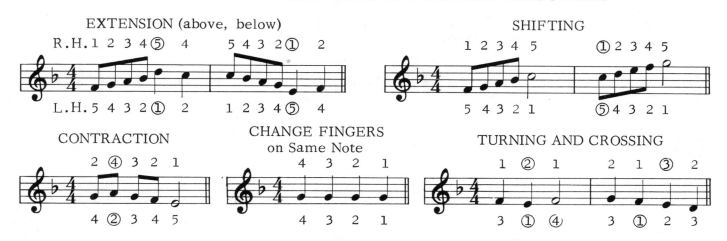

EXTENSION (above, below)

SHIFTING

CONTRACTION

CHANGE FINGERS
on Same Note

TURNING AND CROSSING

Song 28. In the treble melody compare the two positions from the lowest note. Practice spacing your fingers to fit these positions on the keys. Identify all the ways of changing position that are needed in this piece. Find a new V_7 chord position in the bass.

28. ONE MORE RIVER

American Spiritual

Skipping tempo, not too fast

WRITTEN ASSIGNMENT FOUR

I. Below each note write the number of beats the note receives. Place measure bars to make the correct number of beats in each measure.

II. Tell the name of the key and write on the staff the keynote indicated by the following key signatures:

Key of _____   Key of _____   Key of _____   Key of _____

III. Write this pattern twice in sequence. Does it sound pleasing on the piano? Add an ending of one to three notes. Does the music sound concluded?

IV. Write these intervals:

up a 4th   down a 2nd   up a 3rd   down a 5th   up a 6th   up an 8th

29. EXERCISE: EXTENSION of FINGERS, from "The Virtuoso Pianist"

Charles Louis Hanon (1820-1900)
(adapted H. R.)

Transpose this exercise. Create different rhythms. Invent similar exercises with an extension between other fingers.

28

ACCIDENTAL—a sharp, flat, or natural (♮) sign foreign to the key signature. The accidental (immediately before a note) affects only the staff degree on which it is written; its duration is for the one measure only.

NATURAL (♮)—cancels previous sharps or flats on that staff degree.

Composition 30 is an orchestral piece, not a song. Why is this piece not in the key of C major? What is the home tone?

PREPARATORY EXERCISES

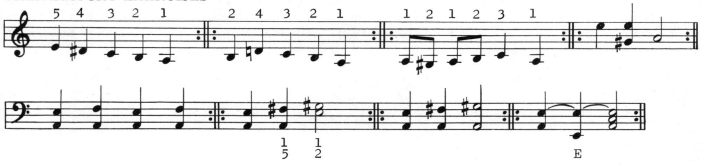

30. Theme from MARCHE SLAVE

Peter I. Tchaikovsky (1840-1893)
(arr. H. R.)

Moderato, marcia funebre

THE STRUCTURE OF MAJOR SCALES

The melodies and chords of most occidental music are based on a scale system.

The basic SCALE (from the word meaning ladder) is a progression of eight tones adhering to a specific formula of steps and half steps. These tones are in successive alphabetical order from one tonic or keynote to the next tonic or name note.

MAJOR SCALE FORMULA or pattern: half steps between degrees (tones) 3–4 and 7–8 and whole steps between all other degrees. Play the C major scale and observe the half steps between white keys E–F (tones 3–4) and B–C (tones 7–8). All scales other than C require sharps or flats to conform to the scale pattern.

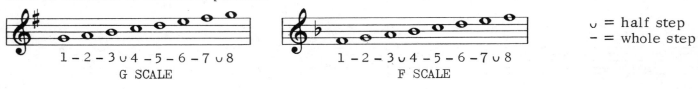

NAMES OF SCALE DEGREES: Tonic (I), Supertonic (II), Mediant (III), Subdominant (IV), Dominant (V), Submediant or Superdominant (VI), Leading Tone (VII).

The scale formula has two identical four-tone patterns or TETRACHORDS separated by a whole step. Tetrachord fingering: L.H., 4 3 2 1 (or 5 4 3 2); R.H., 1 2 3 4 (or 2 3 4 5).

Play scales and chant steps and half steps. Play the D scale, E scale, and others.

Fingering for scales C, G, D, A, and E, ascending:
R.H.—1 2 3 1 2 3 4 5   L.H.—5 4 3 2 1 3 2 1   To descend:
(turn thumb under)   (turn 3rd over thumb)   Read the numbers backward.

Write several scales, marking the steps and half steps between tones.

HARMONIZE the tones of the scale; play a chord with each tone of the scale. Use a chord that contains the scale note, or experiment by ear to find a suitable chord.

Song 31. Observe the scale line in this carol; use correct scale fingering. Play the dotted rhythm by ear. Transpose into the keys of D major and E major. You may wish to harmonize the song.

31. JOY TO THE WORLD

George Frederick Handel (1685–1750)
Words, Isaac Watts

30

SERIES OF MAJOR SCALES

SHARP SCALES. Each new sharp scale in the series begins on the fifth tone (second tetrachord) of the preceding scale, and is therefore five tones higher than its predecessor. The new scale retains the sharp(s) from the old scale, and adds a sharp on the seventh tone of the new scale. Test this formula on the keyboard.

FLAT SCALES. Each new flat scale in the series begins on the fourth tone of the preceding scale, and is therefore four tones higher than its predecessor. The new scale retains the flat(s) from the preceding scale, and adds a flat on the fourth tone of the new scale. Try this on the keyboard.

Notice that three of the scales have ENHARMONIC EQUIVALENTS (the same tones with different names). Which of these scales do you think would be used more often?

Various fingerings are used for scales. In all scales you must anticipate where the thumb is to turn under the fingers. The following fingering is traditional.

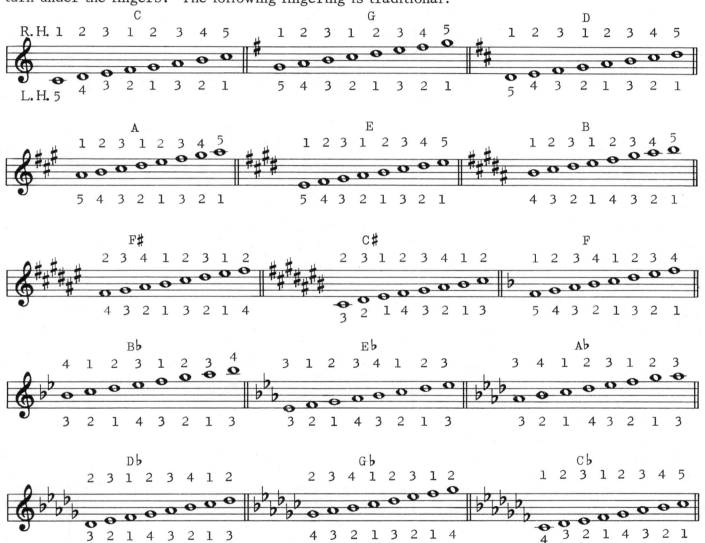

Song 32. Use correct fingering for the scale line throughout the song.

32. THE FIRST NOEL

With spirit   French

The __ first __ No - el, the __ An - gel did say, Was to cer - tain poor
In __ fields __ where __ they lay __ keep-ing their sheep On a cold win-ter's

Continued. Practice turning the page.

shep-herds in fields as they lay; No - el,____ No - el, No -
night____ that was____ so deep.

el, No - el, Born is the King____ of Is - ra - el.

FERMATA or "bird's eye." Hold longer than the time value of the note.

CLAP and COUNT:

Song 33. Find the scale line in the melody. Supply chords where harmony is missing. List the notes in chords I, IV, and V₇. On beat "1" of each measure write and play a chord containing some of the melody notes of that measure.

33. BELIEVE ME, IF ALL THOSE ENDEARING YOUNG CHARMS

Irish

32

THE STRUCTURE OF CHORDS

A chord can be constructed on any tone of the scale. The <u>primary chords</u> (used most often) are built on the first, fourth, and fifth tones ("degrees") of the scale. See Ex. (i).

Chords take their name from the scale tone on which they are built. Chords are referred to by Roman numerals (I, IV, V), by scale degree name (tonic, subdominant, dominant), or by letter name (C chord, F chord, G chord). See Ex. (ii).

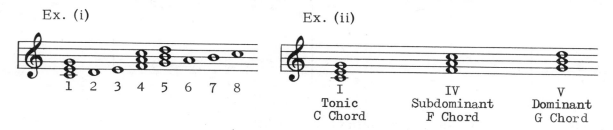

Three-tone chords or TRIADS consist of a ROOT (tone on which the chord is constructed), a THIRD (an interval of a third above the root), and a FIFTH (an interval of a fifth above the root). See Ex. (iii). The notes are an interval of a third apart. Read chord notes upward from the lowest note.

If we add an interval of a third on top of a dominant chord (V), we have a dominant seventh (V_7) chord. The added note creates an interval of a seventh from the root to the top note. See Ex. (iv). This is a four-note chord when complete but is often used in incomplete form — with the fifth omitted. See Ex. (v) above. Play these examples.

When a chord is in root position, the root of the chord is at the bottom. For easy playing, chords IV and V are inverted (rearranged) in easy position (close to the position of the tonic chord). You have been playing chords in easy position. Here, notes "common to" two chords (contained in both I and IV, or in I and V_7), are played by the same finger; other notes are so near that only slight finger shifts are required. The 5th of Chord I is the same note as the root of Chord V or V_7. The root of Chord I is the same note as the 5th of Chord IV. Study and play Example (vi).

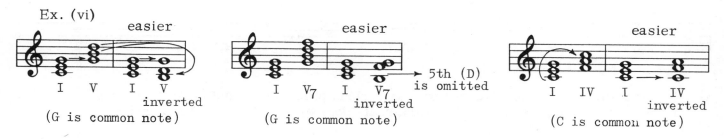

Play chords I, IV, and V_7 in root position in several keys.

Write the tonic, subdominant, and dominant seventh chords in root position, and label each chord.

CHORDING OR STRUMMING AN ACCOMPANIMENT

A simple informal accompaniment can be provided without playing the melody. The right hand plays the chords, the left hand plays the chord root on an accented beat. This type of accompaniment should suit the meter and style of the song.

Sing the melody and <u>chord</u> an accompaniment for "Oh! Susanna" (p. 25) and for "Ach Du Lieber Augustin," below. Another person may play the melody an octave higher, in duet.

On the first repetition in Song 34, omit the 1st ending $\boxed{1.}$ and use the 2nd ending $\boxed{2.}$. Remember to repeat the two measures preceding the D.C. sign.

34. ACH DU LIEBER AUGUSTIN

CREATIVE MUSIC WRITING

I. Early Byzantine music was constructed by stringing together some standard melodic formulas. Can you make two different tunes, using only the following patterns in a different order? You might try harmonizing your tunes.

II. Use the following three-note pattern, at various pitch levels and in reverse (e.g., A-G-F), to make a melody. On what tone of the scale does a composition usually end?

III. Write an "answer" to this musical "question":

BROKEN-CHORD ACCOMPANIMENT

In a "broken" chord, not all the tones are played simultaneously. Play these chords solid or "block" style first, then broken.

Block   Broken

PEDAL. The damper pedal (on the right) releases the dampers from the strings and allows the strings to continue to vibrate. Push the pedal down, hold, and lift the foot according to the sign

⌊⎯⎯⎯⎯⎯⎯⎯⎯⎯⎯⎯⎯⎯⎯⎯⌋ . While using the pedal, keep your heel on the floor.
down   up

Song 35. Practice the bass part first as block chords, then broken as written in WALTZ STYLE. Where does the melody extend above and below the five-finger pattern? Practice this extension, noticing the widest interval. Accent beat "1" slightly. Observe the change of clef.

35. DU, DU LIEGST MIR IM HERZEN

German

36. CONTRARY MOTION

In contrary motion, the notes for each hand progress in opposite directions. Find an example of contrary motion in "Polly Wolly Doodle." Compare the phrases and observe the shifting finger positions.

37. POLLY WOLLY DOODLE

American

Lively

Oh I went down South for to see my Sal, Sing Polly wolly doodle all day; My Sal she is a spun-ky gal, Sing Polly wolly doodle all day. Fare thee well, Fare thee well, Fare thee well my fai-ry fay; For I'm goin' to Louisi-ana for to see my Susy-anna, Sing Polly wolly doodle all day.

CLAP and COUNT:
(Maintain a steady beat!)

Can you find any of these
rhythms in Song 38?

Song 38 is in the DORIAN MODE, one of the Ecclesiastical Modes used in the Middle Ages before our modern scale was adopted. D is the "final" note (tonic); only the white keys are used.

PREPARATORY EXERCISE:

Finger crossing and thumb turning.

38. EARLY IN THE MORNING

Allegro

Sea Chantey

37

INCOMPLETE CHORDS can provide interesting accompaniment, especially when the missing note is present in the melody. In chords I, IV, and V, the middle note (3rd in the chord) is seldom doubled, to avoid overemphasis. In Songs 39 and 40, analyze the chord harmony, including the treble melody note which is sounded with the chord. In most measures of Song 40, the two bass chords are part of the same chord.

39. MY LORD, WHAT A MORNIN'

Spiritual

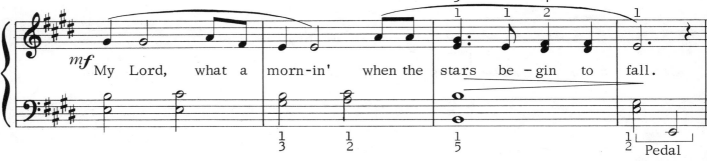

Transpose Song 39 into the key of E flat major by using B flat, E flat, and A flat in the key signature.

Song 40. Play through the 1st ending ⌐1.⌐ ; repeat from the beginning and play the 2nd ending, omitting the 1st. Repeat the two measures between repeat signs (the last 2 measures on the page). For the final repetition (Da capo) play only the 2nd ending. Observe the shift of a finger in measure 1.

40. LONG, LONG AGO

Thomas H. Bayley

38

In PARALLEL MOTION the notes for two voices or hands move in the same direction. Find parallel motion in Song 41. Observe the key signature. To read chords quickly, notice any repeated notes. Play the lower note of these chords and observe the COUNTERMELODY (against the melody).

41. DRINK TO ME ONLY WITH THINE EYES

English
Words, Ben Jonson

MUSICAL FORM

Form is the structure or design of music. A phrase is the unit of structure in most songs (see p. 18). Songs are generally in two-part or in three-part song form.

THREE-PART SONG FORM, also called "A B A FORM" (but most often actually A A B A).
Analyze Song 41 in this form.

- A—The first phrase.
- A—The second phrase is an exact repetition of the first.
  - In many songs the second phrase, called A prime or A', is repeated with some alteration. See "Lightly Row," p. 18.
- B—The third phrase introduces a different idea and provides variety.
- A—The fourth phrase is like A (or A' as in "Lightly Row"). The repetition provides unity and balance in the song.

TWO-PART SONG FORM, also called "A B."
Both parts may be repeated but A is never the final part.

Recognition of like and similar phrases aids sight reading and technical accuracy.

Analyze the form of the following songs: 11, p.12; 16, p.18; 22, p.22; 23, p.24; 28, p. 27; 33, p.32; 39, p.38. Many songs are more irregular and therefore more difficult to classify.

Song 42. Observe that another type of broken chord is used in this accompaniment.

42. ON WINGS OF SONG

Felix Mendelssohn (1809-1847)
(arr. H. R.)

What scale tones are in the bass figure? This repeated figure suggests tramping feet.

43. WHEN THE SAINTS GO MARCHING IN

Traditional

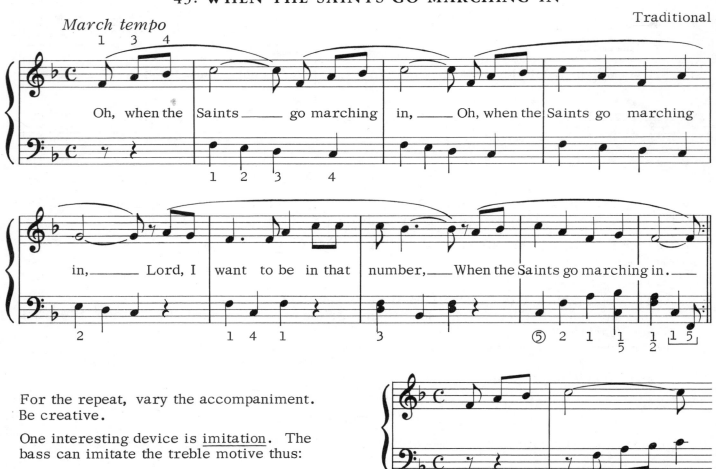

Oh, when the Saints ___ go marching in, ___ Oh, when the Saints go marching

in, ___ Lord, I want to be in that number, ___ When the Saints go marching in. ___

For the repeat, vary the accompaniment. Be creative.

One interesting device is <u>imitation</u>. The bass can imitate the treble motive thus:

CANON—a composition in two or more voice parts that employs a strict form of imitation.

44. LITTLE CANON

Konrad Kunz (1812-1875)
(adapted H. R.)

Song 45. Block the bass chords; use the 4th finger on B flat to save the 5th for low F. Find Chord V inverted and Chord V_7 in root position. Keep the left-hand 2nd finger over D for two chords, last staff measures 2-3. Practice the melody "I'm going back to see."

45. THE YELLOW ROSE OF TEXAS

Don George
(arr. H. R.)

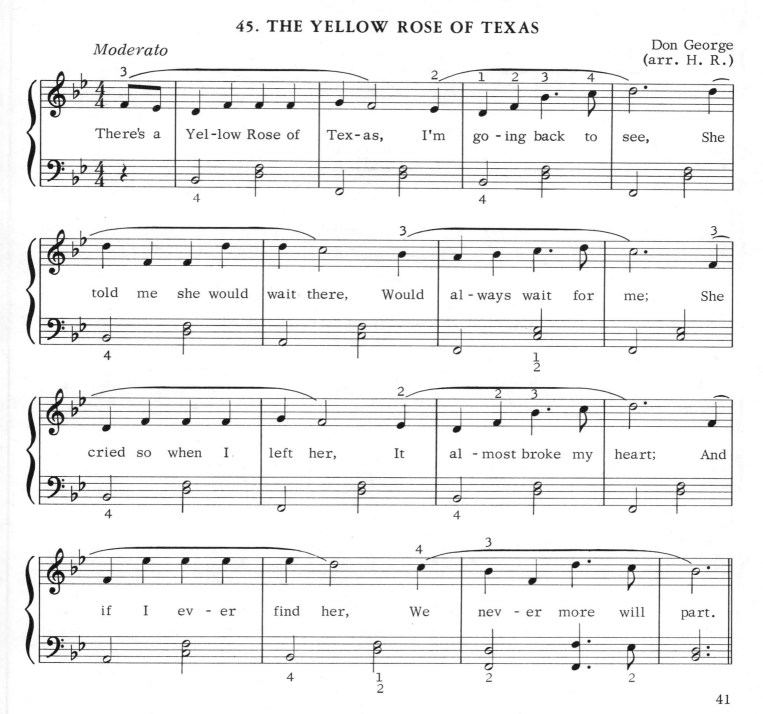

There's a Yel-low Rose of Tex-as, I'm go - ing back to see, She told me she would wait there, Would al-ways wait for me; She cried so when I left her, It al-most broke my heart; And if I ev - er find her, We nev - er more will part.

OSTINATO—a constantly recurring melodic figure, usually in the bass. Experiment with variations of the rhythm and notes in Composition 46.

46. A BIT OF BOOGIE BASS

Animato

H. R.

47. ROVING FINGERS in Irish Dance Style

Presto

H. R.

STACCATO—disconnected tones, marked with a dot above or below each note (♩ = ♪ 𝄽). Fore-arm staccato, from the elbow, is easiest.

GAVOTTE—a folk dance of French origin, starting on beat 3 in moderate $\frac{4}{4}$ time.

PRIMO and SECONDO—the duet parts for a first and second player, respectively.

Piece 48. Find parallel motion. Analyze the bass chord outline. Carefully follow staccato and legato markings. For accuracy, prepare fingers over the correct keys for all the notes in a grouping or unit (all the notes you can reach without changing finger position). Quickly prepare the next position. Notice where hands play opposite key colors. Count aloud. After you learn one part, exchange parts.

48. GAVOTTE from BALLET CÔMIQUE DE LA REINE

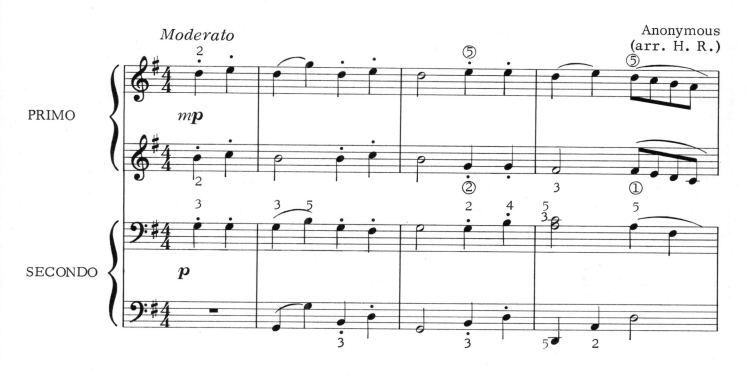

WRITTEN ASSIGNMENT FIVE

I. Add one note to give each measure the correct number of beats.

II. Write waltz-style accompaniment that corresponds with the Roman numerals. (See p. 35.)

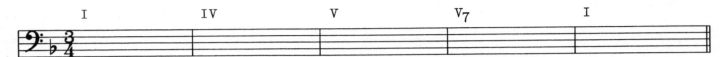

III. On the treble staff write notes that sound well in parallel motion to the notes given on the bass staff. Test the sound on the piano.

IV. Write these intervals:

     up a 5th   down a 4th   up a 2nd   up a 3rd   down a 5th   up a 6th

V. What keys are indicated by the following key signatures:

    Key of ___   Key of ___   Key of ___   Key of ___

VI. Write the E major and A flat major scales without key signatures. Place sharps or flats before (on the line or space of) the notes they are to affect. Label the half steps.

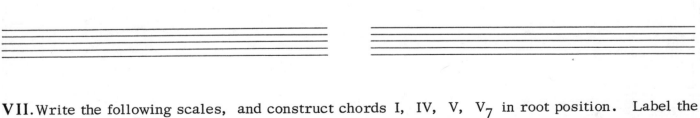

VII. Write the following scales, and construct chords I, IV, V, V₇ in root position. Label the chords.

Scale of B major   Scale of E flat major

SUGGESTIONS FOR SIGHT READING

I. Preliminary Analysis

1. Rhythm. Check the time signature, kinds of notes and rests, and rhythm patterns. Clap and count the complex patterns or the entire song.
2. Tonality and finger-key position. Check the key signature (touch the black keys); find the keynote and the starting position on the keys; look for changes of position; identify the highest and lowest notes and any unfamiliar notes.
3. Design. Compare the phrases; identify the melody patterns (scale line or chord outline); identify the accompaniment style—chords, parallel and contrary motion.
4. Set your tempo by counting a full preliminary measure (plus any absent beats of the first measure); then, without pause, begin to play.

II. Playing (Sight Reading)

1. Read all the notes in a pattern as one unit, seeing scale lines or chord outlines.
2. Prepare fingers over the correct keys for each pattern or unit ("handful").
3. Play the pattern using the finger that lies over the proper key.
4. Look ahead for new patterns and positions.
5. Watch the music; try not to look at your hands or the keys.
6. Keep going and maintain a steady rhythm; do not stop to "correct" mistakes.

49. SHOEMAKER DANCE

Danish

SUGGESTIONS FOR EFFICIENT PRACTICE

1. Obtain a general concept of the music by hearing it, if possible.
2. Analyze the music. See "Preliminary Analysis" above.
3. Play through the music to discover difficult passages; mark these for special work.
4. To master the difficult passages, concentrate on the KINESTHETIC PATTERNS used.
   a. Practice silent preparation of fingers (covering the keys) for each position needed for a group of notes in a pattern, recognizing scale and chord lines, interval spacing, and any black keys, and the best fingering for high and low notes. Play this pattern in rhythm a few times. Practice shifting to the position of the next pattern. Repeat.
   b. To improve slow coordination of particular fingers on particular keys, play each pair of fingers back and forth rapidly (tremolo) on their keys.
   c. To improve coordination of the two hands, practice a pattern or short unit with each hand alone until up to tempo; practice the unit with hands together slowly and then gradually faster until the desired tempo is reached.
5. Play the entire composition, giving attention to the musical expression.
6. Always use correct fingering to make the muscular pattern a habit as soon as possible. Practice as slowly as necessary to prevent making mistakes or having to "unlearn."

This composition MODULATES or changes keys. Play the five-finger pattern in each key used.
Observe the changing clef signs and the accidentals (see p. 29). Identify the treble notes on
leger lines. Practice changing positions in measures 2, 7, 10, and 15. In measure 3 keep the
left thumb over G, ready to return. Observe the crescendo markings. In $\frac{6}{8}$ time 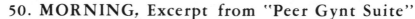 = 1 beat.

50. MORNING, Excerpt from "Peer Gynt Suite"

Edvard Grieg (1843-1907)
(arr. H. R.)

The PENTATONIC SCALE has only five tones. One form, without half steps, can be played using only the black keys of the piano. This form is found in early musical cultures in China, Polynesia, and Africa, and also in American Indian, Celtic, and Scottish music. This scale may sound major when F sharp or G flat is the tonic, or minor when E flat or D sharp is the tonic.

Try to improvise an Oriental-type melody in the pentatonic scale on the black keys. Pieces using only black keys are easy to play. No keys sound wrong in any order!

The next piece conveys the solemnity and beauty that Indians expressed in their songs about nature. The music suggests the dipping of paddles from a birch canoe that glides by and disappears in the distance. The drum effect of the open fifths must be only a light accompaniment.

8va—Play the note an octave lower; or, if above a note, play an octave higher. Dots after the 8va (8va. . . . .) indicate the length of time it is to be applied.

51. LAND OF THE SILVER BIRCH

Canadian
(arr. H. R.)

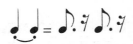

PORTATO—slightly disconnected tones, neither legato nor staccato.

In the first section of Piece 52, the accompaniment figure is made of chord tones. To discover which chords are used, block (play simultaneously) the two bass notes in each beat, along with the melody note. Find the bass sequence in the first staff. Play sixteenth notes evenly, four to a beat; count "1 & 2 &." Practice the scale pattern.

52. FIDDLE TUNE

American
(arr. H. R.)

Write the second phrase (2nd grand staff) of "Fiddle Tune" transposed one step higher.

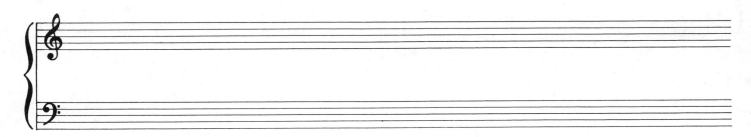

INVERSIONS

The tones of any chord can be arranged in different orders, which are called inversions. In root position (1-3-5 or do-mi-sol order) the root is at the bottom. Put the root at the top, and start on "3" of the chord; this order is first inversion. For the second inversion, put the lowest note of the first inversion at the top, and start on "5" of the chord. Play the C major tonic chord in all these positions.

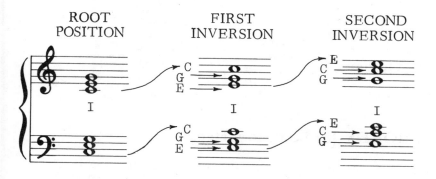

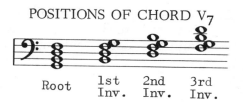

In the 3rd Inversion, the 7th of the chord is at the bottom.

To identify a chord that is inverted, find the root by rearranging the notes into root position (1-3-5 order), in which the notes have interval distances of thirds. Observe the interval spacing in the inversions; play and count the intervals of the notes from the lowest note of each inversion.

Rapid recognition of chord outlines, including inversions, will aid reading and technique. Play and name the chords and inversions in the following exercise. Since inversions are basic in some common types of accompaniment, practice the exercise until the fingers memorize the shifting positions, and transpose the exercise into other keys.

53. EXERCISE: INVERSIONS of CHORDS

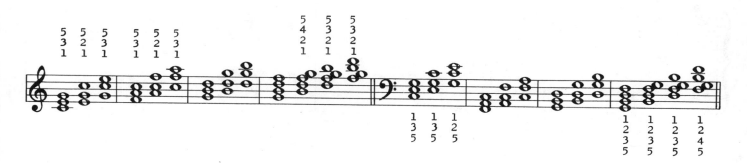

Many pieces begin with the melodic intervals of the tonic chord in second inversion. Sing the familiar melodies "Taps," "Clementine," and "Auld Lang Syne," and find two different positions of the tonic chord outlined in each melody. Can you play these melodies by ear?

WRITTEN ASSIGNMENT SIX

1. Construct the tonic chord in the key of G major in root position and both inversions.
2. Construct the IV chord in the key of F major in root position and both inversions.
3. Construct the V_7 chord in the key of D major in root position and all inversions.
4. List the Roman numeral and the position (root or specific inversions) of the chords given here.

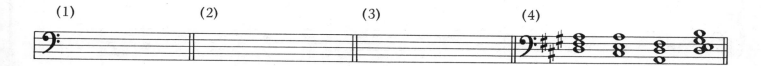

Identify each inversion of the C, F, and G major and G₇ chords (either block or broken) in this piece.

PREPARATORY EXERCISES

1. Plan the interval spacing of the fingers for each chord unit; silently touch the keys of this unit; anticipate the finger spacing for the next unit; swiftly move to the new position and touch the keys silently.

2. Provide for smooth connection of the units by playing the first note of the unit alone and the next two notes simultaneously, making the entire passage legato.

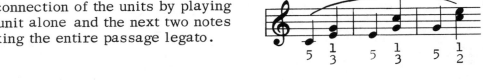

54. GALLOPING CHORDS (broken, inverted)

Cornelius Gurlitt (1820-1901)
(adapted H. R.)

In this aria observe the ALBERTI BASS, a type of repeated broken-chord bass figure named after the composer. Find chord inversions in the bass and in the treble parts. Learn the rhythm of each hand separately, counting and playing. Count and clap:

4 an–d   1   & 2 an–d 3   & 4 an–d   1   & 2 & 3 &

55. Theme from THE MARRIAGE OF FIGARO (Optional)

Wolfgang A. Mozart (1756-1791)

(arr. H. R.)

CADENCES

A cadence is the close of a phrase. In an <u>authentic</u> <u>cadence</u> the active dominant seventh chord in root position <u>resolves</u> to the passive or restful tonic chord in root position. The V_7 chord contains the most active tones of the scale, 4 and 7, which normally "pull" toward their nearest restful tones a half step distant, tones 3 and 8 respectively. Find both of these active tones in the V_7 chords illustrated; find the passive tones to which they resolve in the tonic chord. If the soprano (highest note) of the tonic chord is also a root tone, the cadence is called a <u>perfect</u> <u>cadence</u>. Find the perfect authentic cadence in the following exercises. Be able to play these cadences by memory in all of the common keys.

56. EXERCISE: CADENCES

The left hand should also practice chord progressions written for the right hand in Exercise 56.

PASSING TONES and NEIGHBOR TONES. A chord outline may be the basis of a melody, with nonharmonic notes between some chord tones, In example (i), C, F, and A are tones of the tonic chord; G is a passing tone (P.T.) between chord tones F and A. In example (ii), C and F are tones of the tonic chord; E is a neighbor tone of F (the melody visits a neighbor and then returns). Fast music readers recognize chord outlines, prepare kinesthetic patterns (spacing of fingers) to fit the chord intervals on the keys, and learn to "tuck in" the filler notes.

Analyze the chord outlines in the melody of Song 57, and mark the passing tones and neighbor tones. The blank bass staves are for writing chords. (You may wish to wait until you have studied additional suggestions for harmonization, including secondary chords and octave swing bass.)

57. HOME ON THE RANGE

SYNCOPATION

In SYNCOPATED RHYTHM the accents in the measure are "misplaced." Normally beat "1" and the first beat of the last half of the measure are accented. Syncopation breaks this rule. Observe that long notes seem strong, short notes seem weak.

Find syncopation in Song 58. In measures with divided beats, clap and count: 1 & 2 & 3 & 4 &.
CHROMATIC refers to the movement of tones by half steps. Find chromatic progressions in Song 58.

Compare the phrases of Song 58. Observe that the same theme or melody is used throughout, and that some notes (G's) are decorated in the first measure of the last two staves. Do you find chromatic neighbor notes and chord intervals in the decoration?

To shift the left hand accurately (last bass staff, measures 1–2), practice two notes at a time, pairing beats 1 and 2, beats 3 and 4. When are the notes in the pair both black, both white, or one white and one black?

58. STANDING IN THE NEED OF PRAYER

COUNTERPOINT

Counterpoint literally means point against point or melody against melody. A melody is not harmonized with chords, but is accompanied by another melody or melodies in which each voice part (such as soprano, alto, tenor, bass) is independent. In instrumental music the parts also are called voice parts. The simplest type of counterpoint is the round or canon, such as we played on pages 22 and 41.

The following minuet is not in strict counterpoint, but since it does not have chordal harmony, it provides an easy introduction to music that moves in two voice parts. Notice the occurrence of both parallel and contrary motion, as well as oblique motion, in which one voice part moves up or down while the other remains on the same pitch level.

Ritardando (rit.) and rallentando (rall.) both indicate that the tempo is to slacken gradually.

59. MINUET IN G

Johann Sebastian Bach (1685-1750)

Continued

Look for syncopation, sequences, and contrary and parallel motion in the next piece.

60. AFTER THE SUNSET

Vivace

Czech
(arr. H. R.)

THE MINOR MODE

The minor mode sounds different from the major mode because the scale pattern is different. In the pure or natural form of the minor mode the half steps are between tones 2-3 and 5-6.

Review the D major scale to compare it with the D minor scale. Do you see why the key signatures are different?

D Minor Scale
1 2 ᴗ3 4 5 ᴗ6 7 8

Chords
I IV

I IV IV

Song 61. Observe the upbeat, and find syncopation. In the last bass measure, while holding D with the 2nd finger, silently shift the thumb onto D, getting ready for the octave. Practice the left-hand notes on the last staff and the preceding measure. To compare the character of minor and major, try this song in major by playing all C's and F's as sharps.

61. WAYFARING STRANGER

American

Adagio

p I'm just a poor way-far-ing stran-ger, a-trav'-ling thro' this world of

woe; but there's no sick-ness, toil nor dan-ger in that bright world to which I

go. I'm go-ing there to see my fa-ther, I'm go-ing there no more to

roam; I'm just a - go-ing o-ver Jor-dan, I'm just a - go-ing o-ver home.

56

RELATIVE MINOR

Every major scale has a relative minor scale, which uses the same key signature but begins on the sixth degree of the major scale.

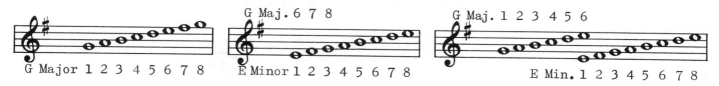

Because the last note of a song or a song section is usually the keynote, it is often a cue revealing whether the song is major or minor. An occasional song uses both the major and the relative minor. Find both in Song 62.

Observe the $\frac{3}{8}$ METER in this song.

62. WE THREE KINGS OF ORIENT ARE

Processional tempo

John H. Hopkins

COMPARISON OF MAJOR AND MINOR CHORDS

In minor pieces chords I and IV are minor. In the natural minor mode (page 56), often a major chord III is used (the tonic of the relative major key). The player should know how to construct major and minor chords. The size of the interval from the root to the 3rd determines the mode.

Compare:

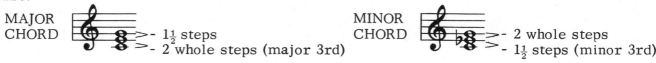

MAJOR CHORD — 1½ steps — 2 whole steps (major 3rd)

MINOR CHORD — 2 whole steps — 1½ steps (minor 3rd)

To make a major chord into a minor chord, lower the third a half step. To make a minor chord into a major chord, raise the third a half step. Try this with several chords.

CHORDING ACCOMPANIMENTS IN MINOR KEYS
Chords for Song 63 (Key of A Minor)

Sing the following tune (or someone can play it an octave higher), and chord an accompaniment, using the chords shown. Analyze the inverted chords. The bass notes marking the natural accents on beats 1 and 4 and the chords on beats 3 and 6 give a lilting rhythm suggestive of children skipping. Plan your melody fingering; avoid shifting position within a phrase member.

63. PAT WORKS ON THE RAILWAY

Rollicking

Irish-American

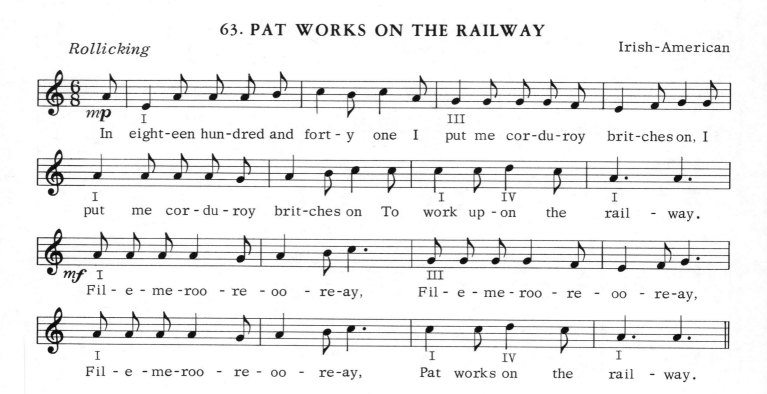

In eight-een hun-dred and fort-y one I put me cor-du-roy brit-ches on, I put me cor-du-roy brit-ches on To work up-on the rail - way.

Fil - e - me-roo - re - oo - re-ay, Fil - e - me-roo - re - oo - re-ay,

Fil - e - me-roo - re - oo - re-ay, Pat works on the rail - way.

In the most frequently used form of the minor mode, the HARMONIC MINOR, the seventh tone of the pure minor scale is raised one half step (by an accidental), thereby creating an interval of a step and a half between tones 6 and 7, and a half step between 7 and 8 (making the 7th a "leading tone" to the tonic). The V and V_7 chords use the raised seventh tone of the scale as the 3rd of the chord and are therefore major chords.

64. GO DOWN, MOSES

The occasionally found MELODIC MINOR in the descending scale conforms to the pure or natural minor scale. The ascending scale deviates from the natural minor; the sixth and seventh degrees are both raised one half step. Play several melodic minor scales.

"Greensleeves" was a ballad known as early as 1575 in England. Since then, the song has had many adaptations, including this famous Christmas carol.

Song 65, in E minor, uses the natural or pure form of the mode, except in a few measures where C sharp and D sharp give a melodic-minor flavor. Analyze the bass chords and practice the shifts in position. In measures 3, 7, 9, 11, 13, and 15, use the thumb as a pivot to transfer to the new position. Find and practice the octave intervals. Practice the right-hand transfer of the 3rd finger over the thumb, and reach the thumb down quickly for its next key in measures 10 and 14.

65. WHAT CHILD IS THIS?

Old English Melody ("Greensleeves")

What forms of the minor mode are used in these Jewish songs?

66. OH HANUKAH

67. ELI ELI

68. BALALAIKA (Refrain)

MINOR SCALES (Harmonic form)

Write the descending scale (and fingering) in each key. Write the name of the related major key.

Play these OCTAVE CHORDS in both solid and broken styles. Transpose into several keys.

69. OLD SMOKY

Slowly   American

Composition 70. Where is an octave chord outlined in the melody? What is its root? Listen to a recording of this composition; what instruments play this theme?

70. Theme from SYMPHONY NO. 6, "PASTORALE" (Optional)

Allegretto   Ludwig van Beethoven (1770-1827)

Block the broken-chord bass. Practice the left-hand leaps from measures 1 to 3, comparing the color of keys played by each finger. Compare the color of the left-hand keys in measures 1–2 and 3–4 after the double bar. Play the right-hand notes, measure 2, several times—blocked and as written; how far apart are the highest and lowest notes? How many times does this pattern occur in the song?

71. OH, DEAR, WHAT CAN THE MATTER BE?

English

72. VELOCITY STUDY A

Karl Czerny (1791-1857)
(adapted H. R.)

Continued

GRACE NOTE or acciaccatura—an ornamental note "crushed" against the principal note. Observe the smallness of the note, the diagonal dash, and the slur. Play the note very close to the principal note. When the grace note occurs with a chord, it may be sounded simultaneously and immediately released.

Song 73. The grace note with the open fifth creates a bagpipe effect. In the Alberti bass, chord roots on the accented beat "1" make a strong progression. Compare the phrases of this song.

73. THE GALWAY PIPER

Irish

Song 74. Do all the phrases have the same number of measures? In the next to the last treble measure, observe the substitution of the 5th for the 4th finger to maintain legato.

74. COME, THOU ALMIGHTY KING

Felice de Giardini (1716-1796)

75. VELOCITY STUDY B

Karl Czerny (1791-1857)
(adapted H. R.)

76. RAGE OVER THE LOST PENNY

In the next piece, which phrases have a contrapuntal bass and which phrases have chordal accompaniment? Observe the repeated note patterns and the sequences in either hand; find repeated finger patterns. As preparatory exercises, practice the sequences in the first staff with each hand separately, using correct fingering. Block all the bass chords in the third staff. Find passing tones and neighbor tones in the melody (see p. 52).

77. COUNTRY GARDENS

English

SECONDARY CHORDS IN MAJOR KEYS

Chords II, III, and VI are minor. Their lower interval is a minor 3rd—one and a half steps.

Chord VII is diminished. Its two minor 3rds form an interval of a <u>diminished</u> (shrunken) 5th.

Chords II and VI have notes in common with Chord IV and are often substituted for IV. Chords VI and III have notes in common with Chord I and are sometimes substituted for I.

Chord II also has notes in common with Chord V_7 and can sometimes be substituted for Chord V_7. Chord II, the most frequently used of the secondary chords, often serves as a dominant of Chord V, especially when the 3rd of II is raised, making it a major II. See this usage of Chord II in "Country Gardens" (p. 68), third staff, next to the last measure.

Chord VII is often considered an incomplete V_7 (with the root missing). Its active tones resolve to the nearest passive tones.

SECONDARY CHORDS IN MINOR KEYS

In harmonic minor keys, primary chords I and IV are minor, V_7 is major. Secondary chord VI is major; II and VII are diminished. Chord III is <u>augmented</u>; its lower 3rd is major and its upper 3rd is major. These two major 3rds create an augmented or expanded 5th.

By means of accidentals, chords on other tones of the major or minor scale may be made into diminished or augmented chords. For example, the inverted tonic chord in the following theme is converted into an augmented chord (D♭–F–A♮).

78. Theme from the NEW WORLD SYMPHONY

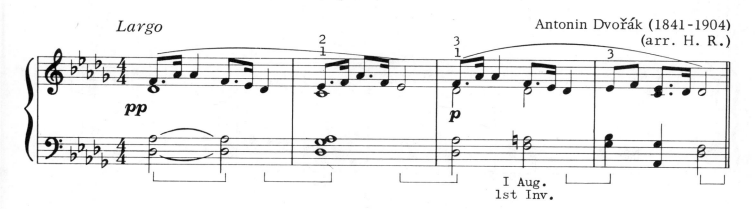

This music shifts back and forth between the minor and major modes. How many sections of each do you find? In the first measure of each section, indicate whether the section is major or minor. Find a VI chord and several II chords. The chord before the VI chord is the dominant seventh of that chord; mark it V₇ of VI.

79. COME BACK TO SORRENTO

Italian
(arr. H. R.)

THE PEDAL

Legato tones can be produced by finger connections and substitutions, by transferring arm weight, and by pedaling. The use of the damper pedal, on the right, to sustain tones and overtones, helps to increase the sonority of the music. Change the pedal for clarity of melody, harmony, rhythm patterns, and phrasing, and for special effects.

LEGATO PEDAL or SYNCOPATED PEDAL. On the first note, push the key and the pedal simultaneously. Thereafter, play the key and instantly release the pedal to stop the vibration of former tones; immediately push the pedal down again to catch the new tone before the vibrations begin to fade. As you do the following exercise, chant: "play (the key), up-down (the foot)."

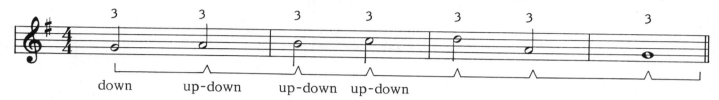

down   up-down   up-down   up-down

$\frac{2}{2}$ METER—a half note receives one beat.

80. JACOB'S LADDER

Andante   Traditional

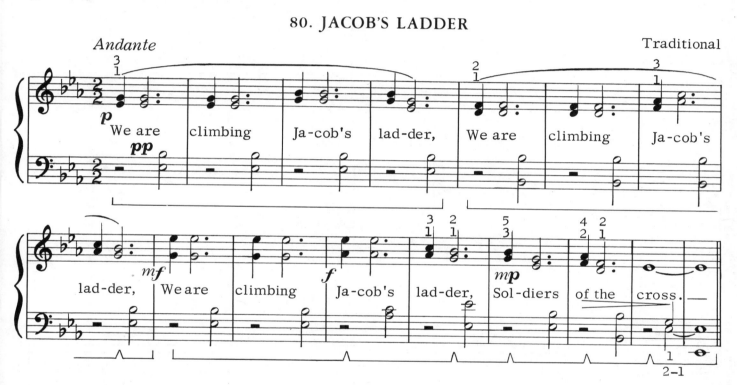

We are climbing Ja-cob's lad-der, We are climbing Ja-cob's lad-der, We are climbing Ja-cob's lad-der, Sol-diers of the cross.

The Schumann "choral" (hymn) should be played reverently.

81. EIN CHORAL (Rejoice, O My Soul)

Robert Schumann (1810-1856)

M.M. $\downarrow$ = 54

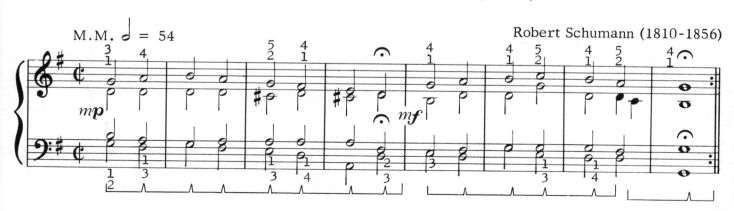

TRIPLET—three notes receive the same time as two notes of the same value. The triplet is written with a slur mark, and usually has the figure 3 over or under it. If triplets occur throughout the piece of music, the figure 3 does not always appear.

In music with constantly recurring crossing of hands, the right-hand notes have stems pointing upward, the left-hand notes have stems pointing downward.

First, practice the broken chords in solid or block style. Anticipate the spacing of the notes, and prepare the fingers on the keys ahead of time to insure accuracy. When a chord is repeated by the same hand, retain the shape of the chord in the hand.

82. ETUDE IN TRIPLETS

H. R.

ROLLED CHORDS often imitate the strumming on small stringed instruments like ukeleles. Roll the chord from the bottom tone to the top tone, smoothly and evenly, keeping the tones soft. The rolled chord is a very fast arpeggio. Notice how the roll is indicated in the music.

Practice the rolled chords in Song 83. Block the successive treble intervals of sixths before practicing the melody.

83. HAWAIIAN NIGHT

Hawaiian

84. EXERCISE: BOUNCING SIXTHS

Review chord inversions. Identify the bass chords and the melodic chord outlines as root position or as a specific inversion. Practice the bass chords in each measure several times to acquire speed. Prepare the fingers on the keys of the first chord; play, and instantly think the "feel" of finger spacing for the next chord; prepare (cover the keys of) this chord; play and continue. Can you identify syncopation in this piece? Find passing tones and neighbor tones.

How fast can you prepare and play each of these measures?

85. RED RIVER VALLEY

Andante

Traditional

Block the two octave-chord patterns and other chord patterns outlined in the bass. Observe the
soprano notes that are held while alto notes are played by other fingers of the same hand.

86. THE HAPPY FARMER

Animato e grazioso

Robert Schumann (1810-1856)

Fine

87. AMERICA

Moderately

Henry Carey
(arr. H. R.)

88. THE STAR SPANGLED BANNER

J. S. Smith (1750-1836)
(arr. H. R.)

With spirit

89. AMERICA THE BEAUTIFUL

Samuel A. Ward
(arr. H. R.)

Majestically

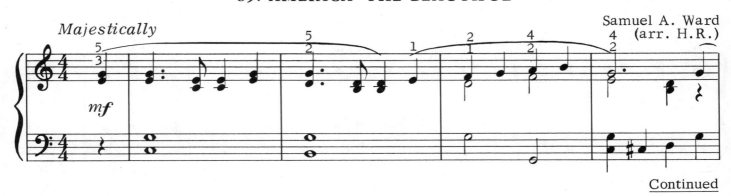

Continued

The Chopin Prelude will be a challenge at this time. You might like to learn a small portion at a time while you continue to play pieces on later pages. The top note of the rolled treble chord can be played by the left third finger: or, this finger can play the bottom treble note.

90. PRELUDE IN A MAJOR

Frederick Chopin (1810-1849)

Compare, count, and clap these rhythmic patterns:
Divide each beat into four parts to feel the relationship.
(Some players like to count "one-e-an-d.")

What is the form of "Soldier's March"? Compare the phrases quickly, looking for the shape of the melody line.

When reading double notes, remember to read by melodic intervals (distances from the preceding notes), and to observe whether any notes are repeated.

Keep the correct finger securely over the key of the repeated notes. Fingers can get ready for the next notes during the rests.

91. SOLDIER'S MARCH

Robert Schumann (1810-1856)

78

What chord position is outlined in the first phrase (4 measures) of the dance? Do you find a passing tone in this phrase? Identify the notes on leger lines. Notice the pickup. Compare the phrases. Find sequences. Why does one phrase appear to be in the key of A major? Carefully follow all markings in the music to make the structure apparent—the short patterns or motives, the phrase members, and the phrase endings. Which notes are to be played portato, and which notes staccato? To hasten your anticipation of kinesthetic patterns when shifting from one position to the next, you might practice blocking the chordal patterns of the short motives.

92. GERMAN DANCE (Optional)

Franz Joseph Haydn (1732-1809)

93. STUDY IN SCALE VELOCITY

H.R.

Two-note slurs can be played mainly from the wrist, from the elbow, or from the hand knuckles.
For wrist action, elevate the wrist slightly; then as you play the first note, drop the wrist to
key level like a bouncing ball; on the second note lift the wrist (rebound) to the original position.
Fingers must be firm. Do not elevate the shoulders.

94. ETUDE IN BROKEN CHORDS—THE TWO-NOTE SLUR

George F. Handel (1685-1759)
(adapted H. R.)

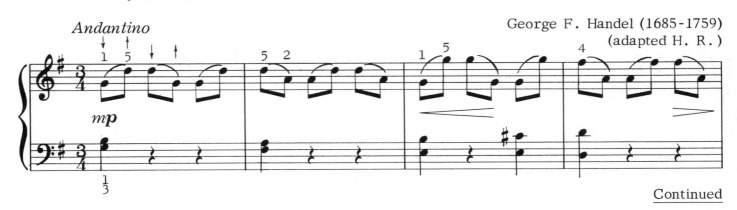

Continued

Mozart composed this minuet when he was only six. Find the triplet. Look for repeated patterns and sequences. Block the outlined chord patterns, observing the intervals. Carefully observe the marks of articulation—slurs, staccato, etc., which help to reveal the musical design.

95. MINUET IN F MAJOR

Wolfgang A. Mozart (1756-1791)

LEARNING A PIECE BY MEMORIZING IT

Hear the piece if possible. Learn the first phrase (4 measures): bass octaves; bass chords, alternating quickly; bass measures. Use the left thumb on the octave as a pivot to shift to a new finger on the same key. Block each treble pattern of this phrase several times, finding two positions in the last pattern; memorize, shifting positions quickly and playing rhythmically. Play both hands together, preparing fingers over the keys of each position. Learn the other phrases in a similar manner, observing similarities of patterns and chords.

96. SWISS YODEL

Alpine Tune
Words, H. R.

SOME WAYS OF IMPROVISING ACCOMPANIMENTS

Before selecting the chords for each measure of a song, list the notes of the principal chords in the key of the song. Remember to include all four notes of the complete V_7 chord. To harmonize the melody, select chords that contain one or more melody notes in the portion of the measure that is being harmonized. If a choice must be made, choose the chord that sounds best. Analyze the melody for passing tones and neighbor tones or other nonharmonic tones that can be ignored in the harmonization.

Block chords can be played on the strong first beat of each measure; new chords are used whenever the harmony needs to change. In slow tempo, chords may occur also on the secondary accent (beat "3" in $\frac{4}{4}$ time, beat "4" in $\frac{6}{8}$ time). Chords need not be played on upbeats.

In general, the voice parts of block-chord progressions should move smoothly, without wide or overlapping leaps. Swing bass (see p. 84) may be used on the piano.

Avoid "doubling" the 3rd of a principal (I, IV, V_7) chord, especially when this note is in the melody. Double the root preferably, or the 5th. In secondary minor chords, doubled 3rds are good.

Omit a chord tone that overlaps a melody tone and causes interference of hands.

To close each phrase (four or eight measures in simple music), use an authentic cadence (V_7–I), or a half-cadence (stopping on V_7 and sounding unfinished), or (but rarely) a plagal (amen) cadence (IV–I). These chords are always in root position. Music usually concludes on an authentic cadence (rarely on a plagal cadence) to end with a feeling of repose. Chord IV should never follow Chord V_7.

When using broken-chord figures, use a portion of the figure or a block chord if a change in harmony does not permit a broken-chord figure to be completed. Use a block chord for the final tonic to contribute to the feeling of conclusion.

The second inversion of a chord is infrequently used except to vary a repeated harmony, or before a V_7 chord in a cadence, when the bass note is the same for both chords. For simple songs in rocking rhythm ($\frac{6}{8}$), a pattern of broken I and V_7 chords may occasionally suffice as accompaniment.

Occasionally a melody note may be harmonized with a chord that has neither the melody note nor notes that normally harmonize with it but which creates an interval of a 6th from the chord root to the melody (e.g., Chord IV for the 2nd tone of the scale, Chord I for the 6th tone).

Types of simple left-hand accompaniments for a melody played by the right hand:

Broken Chords in Easiest Playing Position

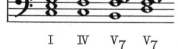

Broken Chords for Different Meters

Broken Chords with Single Notes

Broken Chord Figures

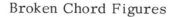

SUGGESTIONS FOR THE ACCOMPANIST

OCTAVES provide louder volume in a large room and add variety to the music. The chord root can be played in octaves in a low bass register on the first beat of each measure. On the following beats, the left hand can play triads in easy position or in other positions, remaining below the melody that the right hand plays. (Complete chords sound too thick and "grumbling" if played lower than the B flat an octave below Middle C.) The melody may be doubled in octaves by the right hand, with other chord tones filled in on accented beats or on strong parts of divided beats, or to emphasize the change of harmony.

In SWING BASS accompaniment, a single low note can be substituted for the octave.

Compose an accompaniment using octaves or swing bass for "The Yellow Rose of Texas," page 41, "Believe Me, If All Those Endearing Young Charms," page 32, "Polly Wolly Doodle," page 36, and "Home on the Range," page 52.

COUNTERMELODY. In an occasional passage you may use contrary motion or intervals of 3rds or 6ths in parallel motion. Parallel 4ths sound dissonant, parallel 5ths sound thin and "open," parallel octaves merely double the same note; all should be avoided in countermelodies and in chord progressions.

INTRODUCTIONS. Introductions set the tempo and can indicate the beginning note for singers. For a very familiar song, however, a single chord may be sufficient if the beginning note of the song is the top note of the chord. For a less well-known song, play an introduction of one or two phrases from the beginning or ending of the song, or the first and last phrases of the song if the arrangement makes the beginning note of the song more apparent to the singers.

Plan an introduction for "Oh! Susanna," page 25, "For He's a Jolly Good Fellow," page 26, and "Du, Du Liegst Mir im Herzen," page 35.

MODULATION. To lead smoothly from a song in one key to a song in a different key the accompanist can use modulation. The most direct way to modulate is to establish the new key by playing a dominant to tonic chord progression in the new key. It is advisable to write these chords to see the smoothest movement of each voice part (soprano, alto, tenor, bass) from one chord to the next. The beginning note of the new song should be given in the upper note of the new tonic chord, in a follow-up chord, or in an introduction.

Write and play modulations from "Roving Fingers in Irish Dance Style," page 42, to "The Yellow Rose of Texas," page 41; and from "Fiddle Tune," page 48, to "Standing in the Need of Prayer," page 53.

TRANSPOSITION. To determine the best key for a song, check the highest and lowest notes and the keynote and find how far the song should be raised or lowered to be within a singing range of D above Middle C to D an octave higher. The easiest transposition to play is a half step higher or lower; the notes may have the same letter names but the key signature will be different (e.g., the key of E major—4 sharps—to the key of E flat major—3 flats). Before playing, examine all accidentals to find the needed changes (e.g., in "On Wings of Song," page 40, the A natural in the key of A flat major would become an A sharp in the key of A major). To transpose one step lower, read all the notes one staff degree lower and use the key signature of the keynote that is one step lower. Accompaniment chords will have the same numerals as in the old key. To transpose up a third, read the notes a third higher or up two staff degrees, from one space to the next space or from one line to the next line.

Leading from the piano is essential for group or community singing, if no conductor is present. The beat must be steady with strong accents from the bass. The volume must not sound forced or shrill and must be suited to the singers' voices; if the accompaniment is too loud, singers respond with strained tones. Dynamics and phrasing are as important in an accompaniment as in a solo.

On the "drum roll" in the introduction, keep firm fingers close to the keys and roll the hand. Make your own accompaniment for this song, using some octaves. Write the notes on the bass staff. See "Octaves" in "Suggestions for the Accompanist," page 84.

97. BATTLE HYMN OF THE REPUBLIC

William Steffe
Words, Julia Ward Howe

Mine eyes have seen the glo - ry of the
He hath loos'ed the fate -ful light-ning of His

1.
com- ing of the Lord; He is tramp - ing out the vin - tage where the
ter - ri-ble swift sword;

2.
grapes of wrath are stored; His truth is march-ing on.

Glo - ry, glo-ry hal-le - lu - jah! Glo - ry, glo-ry hal-le - lu - jah!

Glo - ry, glo-ry hal-le - lu - jah! His truth is march-ing on.

SONGS TO HARMONIZE

Mark the phrasing and fingering for starting a new position on the keys, and also mark the Roman numerals of chords to play. Indicate the style of accompaniment you prefer for each song. On the blank staves, write a folk tune for which a different style of accompaniment is appropriate. Play each piece with more than one kind of accompaniment.

ROSA

THE MAN ON THE FLYING TRAPEZE

Practice the quick leaps from one register of the piano to another. Keep the fingers firm, feeling ready to play the next "handful" of notes. Cover the group of keys for the "handful" of notes.

98. MUSETTE

Johann Sebastian Bach (1685-1750)

♩ —a very short staccato note. (♩ = ♪ 𝄾 𝄾)

99. L'ARABESQUE (Optional)

J. Friedrich Burgmueller (1806-1874)

Allegro scherzando

The contrast of major and minor in this song suggests the sad and happy buffoonery of the clown.

100. THE CLOWN

Fast, with lots of humor

Dmitri Kabalevsky (1904-   )

Play this exercise legato. Practice each hand separately.
Ascending, connect the upper notes of the pairs; descending, connect the lower notes of the pairs.

101. EXERCISE: SCALE in DOUBLE THIRDS

102. A LITTLE SONG

Andantino   Dmitri Kabalevsky (1904-   )

sf or **sfz**–sforzando–a heavy accent on the one note or chord (like cymbals crashing), relative to the volume of the particular passage.

103. Theme from the FIRST SYMPHONY, Finale

Allegro non troppo

Johannes Brahms (1833-1897)
(arr. H. R.)

CANTABILE—singing style

Count the triplets "trip-l-et." Give the exact time value for

Distinguish the melody from the accompaniment, and imitate the mellow tone quality of the horn which plays this theme in the orchestra. Pedal with each bass chord and whenever needed for clarity.

Groups of notes under the slurs or phrasing units tend to build and then to recede in intensity. This effect must not be overdone. Listen to a recording.

104. Theme from the FIFTH SYMPHONY (Optional)

Peter I. Tchaikovsky (1840-1893)

(arr. H. R.)

92

105. EXERCISE: BROKEN CHORDS with INTERVALS of TENTHS

Block the two lower notes of the broken chord, then
the two upper notes. Play the blocks alternately;
swing with a flexible wrist.

106. LULLABY

Tenderly

Johannes Brahms (1833-1897)
(arr. H. R.)

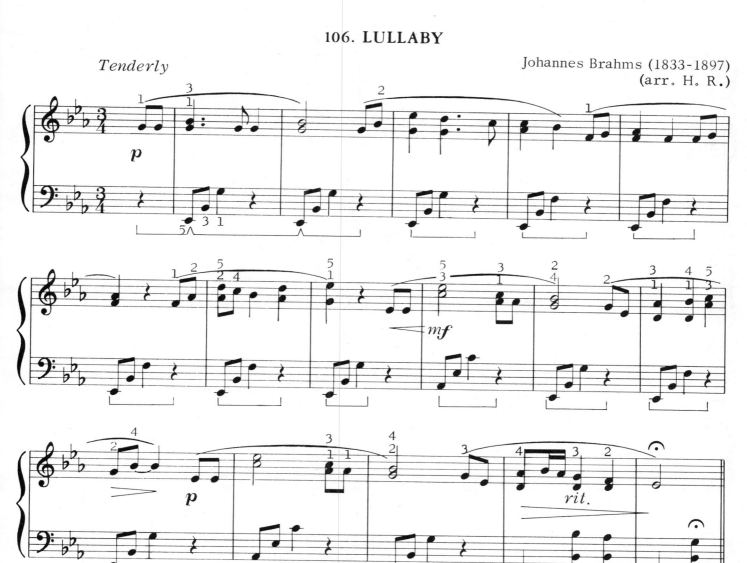

Observe the minor 3rds (1½ step) between any two notes. The following exercise promotes in-
dependence of finger action and extends the reach of the hand. Play it also as a two-octave
arpeggio. Memorize the exercise. Transpose it into several keys. Notice the double flat.

107. EXERCISE: The DIMINISHED SEVENTH CHORD

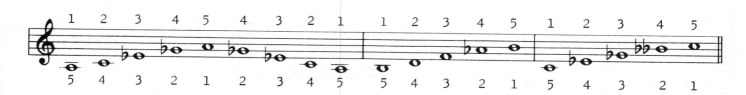

How many broken, inverted diminished seventh chords can you find in this concerto (con-share-toe) theme? Practice blocking the notes of the chord patterns in each measure. The slurred tone groups should flow smoothly.

108. Theme from the SECOND CONCERTO (Optional)

Sergei Rachmaninoff (1873-1943)
(arr. H. R.)

The following short excerpt includes the introduction and ending and two themes from the first movement of the Grieg concerto.

Observe the changes in clef. Notice the triplets. Find diminished seventh chords. Concentrate on kinesthetic patterns to develop speed and accuracy.

109. Theme from the CONCERTO IN A MINOR (Optional)

Edvard Grieg (1843-1907)
(arr. H. R.)

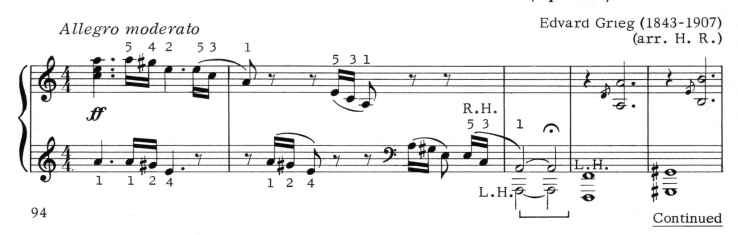

Continued

110. MINUET IN G MINOR (Optional)

Andante con moto

Johann Sebastian Bach (1685-1750)

UNA CORDA (one string)—use the soft pedal on the left; use the damper pedal also, as marked.
TEMPO RUBATO allows the performer to lengthen or shorten some notes slightly for greater
expressiveness. ♩ is a light ACCENT that sustains the note. In Song 111 play the staccato
notes with a tiny bounce from the wrist, keeping firm fingers near the keys; avoid wrist tension.

111. Excerpt from EVENING IN THE COUNTRY

Béla Bartók (1881-1945)

To get the feel of the interval of an octave, practice an exercise in octaves before playing a piece that includes several octave spans.

112. EXERCISE: OCTAVES

PREPARATORY EXERCISES

(measures 1-2)   (measures 5-7) (measure 7)

(measures 5-7)   (measures 1, 3)

113. MINUET IN G, No. 2

Johann Sebastian Bach (1685-1750)

Practice the left hand (last four measures of the second staff) in dotted rhythm and as block octaves, to make the fingers feel secure.

114. ECOSSAISE (Optional)

Allegretto

Ludwig van Beethoven (1770–1827)

This composition by a contemporary of Bach has vitality and a memorable tune. Carefully compare phrases. Concentrate on kinesthetic patterns, intervals, and color of keys. Use a forearm staccato, bouncing from the elbow.

115. Excerpt from THE FIFERS

Francois Dandrieu (1684–1740)

116. EXERCISE: FINGER TWISTER

In songs in two-part harmony, the most common intervals are thirds and sixths. For a legato effect when it is impossible to connect the double notes, connect either the upper notes (preferably) or the lower notes.

117. CARMEN CARMELA

Tempo di Habanera

Mexican

The CHROMATIC SCALE progresses by half steps. Traditional fingering places the third finger on black keys, thumb on single white keys, and thumb and second finger on adjoining white keys E-F and B-C. Play the complete chromatic scale within an octave.

118. CHROMATIC STUDY

Allegro

H. R.

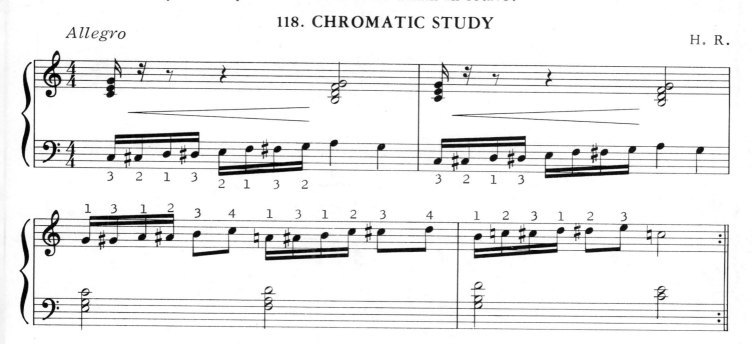

This piece requires beautiful tone quality, legato touch, and legato pedal. For legato repeated notes (in the bass), keep the finger in contact with the key; allow the key to rise to normal position only at the last instant when it must be pressed again. Little pressure is needed if the fingers remain firm and sufficient arm weight is released on each key to produce the desired dynamics. Make the melody tone "sing"; make the accompaniment lighter.

Observe where the thirds in the bass progress chromatically. To learn the feel of this series, play each third only once and then proceed. In the left-hand treble part, how far do the broken sixths progress chromatically? Block these in practice.

119. SONG OF IVAN

Aram Khachaturian (1903-   )

Continued

102

CREATIVE WRITING

Find the PEDAL POINT or ORGAN POINT in the bass of this piece; one note is held while other notes change harmony.

120. TO A WILD ROSE

Edward MacDowell (1861–1908)

Continued

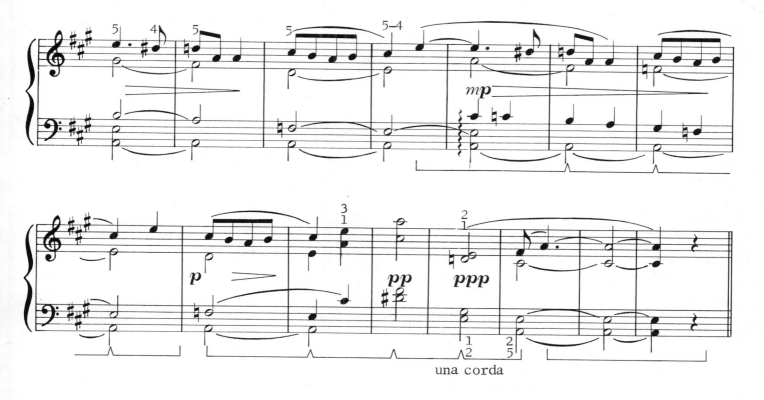

Use a "clinging touch" to make the chords as legato as possible, in flowing style. A slight accent on beat "1" will contribute to the lilt of the waltz. While playing the low bass note, prepare the finger spacing for the higher notes.

121. WALTZ

Andante con moto

Franz Schubert (1797–1828)

GLOSSARY

TEMPO—rate of speed.

  Largo—broadly, very slowly
  Lento—slowly
  Adagio—easily
  Andante—a walking pace
  Andantino—a "little" andante
  Moderato—moderate tempo
  Allegretto—quickly
  Allegro—briskly
  Vivace or Vivo—lively
  Presto—very rapidly
  Prestissimo—as fast as possible

  Changing tempo:
    accelerando, (accel.)—gradual increase in speed
    a tempo—resume the original tempo
    mosso—motion (used with a word indicating more speed or less speed)
    rallentando (rall.)—gradually slowing in speed
    ritardando (rit.)—gradually slowing
    ritenuto (riten.)—immediately slower

DYNAMICS—shading or degrees of intensity or volume for expression.

  pianissimo (pp)—very soft
  piano (p)—soft
  mezzo piano (mp)—moderately soft
  mezzo forte (mf)—moderately loud
  forte (f)—loud
  fortissimo (ff)—very loud

  Changing dynamics:
    crescendo (cresc.)—gradually louder
    decrescendo (decr.)—gradually softer
    diminuendo (dim.)—gradually softer, a small crescendo, a short diminuendo
    sforzando (sf. or sfz)—forced tone or strong accent on the particular note or chord

STYLE

  animato—animated, with spirit
  brio—vigor, spirit
  cantabile—singing style
  dolce—sweetly, delicately
  funebre—funeral
  giocoso—humorously, playfully
  grazioso—gracefully
  legato—smoothly connected tones
  maestoso—majestically
  marcia—march
  pastorale—suggestive of a rural scene
  religioso—with religious feeling
  scherzando—playfully (originally in joking manner)

sostenuto—sustained tones or slightly slower tempo
staccato—disconnected tones

MISCELLANEOUS TERMS

  coda—extra ending on a composition
  con—with
  D. C. (DaCapo)—the beginning, or literally the head
  D. C. al fine—repeat from the beginning to "fine"
  D. S. (Dal Segno)—the sign 𝄋
  D. S. al fine—repeat from the sign to "fine"
  fermata ⌢ —hold the note longer than its time value
  fine (pronounced fee-nay)—the end or finish of a composition
  loco—in regular location or pitch register
  meno—less
  molto—much
  piu—more
  poco—a little
  poco a poco—little by little (gradually)
  sempre—always
  simile—in similar manner
  troppo—too much

SIGNS

  ♯ —sharp
  ♭ —flat
  ♮ —natural
  ⌢ —fermata (see p. 32)

  —repeat sign (see p. 17)

  —repeat sign (see p. 25)

  —tie (see p. 18)

  —slur (see p. 11)

  —endings (see p. 34)

  —pedal sign (see p. 35)

  —staccato (see p. 43)

  —portato (see p. 48)

  —triplet (see p. 72)

  8va . . —see page 47

  > —accent (see p.24)

  —sustained note (see p. 96)

CLASSIFIED INDEX